CONTENTS

PREFACE

According to the American Association of Individual Investors (AAII), if you had invested $1,000 in the stocks of the Standard & Poor's 500 Composite Stock Price Index (S&P 500) at the end of 1940, you would now have more than $791,000 (reinvesting dividends and excluding taxes). The figures are even more dramatic if you had invested the same $1,000 in smaller companies. AAII says your $1,000 would have grown to more than *$4.9 million!* Interesting, but what does that have to do with you? Is it really possible for you to invest and build a fortune?

You bet, and that's what this book is all about. My purpose is to give you the tools you need and show you how you can invest the smart way in stocks, bonds, and mutual funds. The objective is your financial independence. Surprisingly, success does not depend on luck or financial skills. You simply need determination, persistence, and patience.

Why do we invest? Mainly, we invest to secure our financial future. But there are complex choices to make: Should we invest for current income? For capital growth? In what should we invest? Stocks? Bonds? Mutual funds? In what combination? The securities markets are volatile. Successful long-term investing depends on sensible portfolio planning.

You may ask yourself, "What kind of investment portfolio is best suited to *my* needs?" This book responds to that question, provides commonsense principles of intelligent investing, and shows you how to invest the smart way.

Before taking your first investment step, you need a clear destination. What are your objectives? The four most common objectives are financial security, retirement planning, income to meet living expenses, and saving for a child's education. You may be seeking one of these objectives, a combination of these, or perhaps entirely different ones. Whatever your objectives are, they should establish a destination, as well as a chart for measuring your progress. At times, securities markets will turn, and you will be tempted to change direction abruptly. Your objectives should serve as a road map for managing your investment program.

Divided into four parts, *How to Invest the Smart Way in Stocks, Bonds, and Mutual Funds* will give you a lifetime investment strategy that requires only a few hours each month to execute. Part I, "Achieving Financial Independence," shows you how to identify your personal financial objective and outlines the steps you can take to realize it. You will become aware of the risk associated with different types of investments, and I'll give you simple techniques to blunt the tax blow by reducing your taxable capital gains and income distributions.

Part II, "Investing the Smart Way in Stocks," guides you in your quest to realize returns on your invested capital by developing a portfolio of individual stocks that performs above the market averages. As a prudent investor, you will learn to think of stocks as components of a portfolio, rather than as single entities. A diversified group of holdings reduces the overall risk of stocks. Long recognized by sophisticated investors as an important advantage, diversification is often ignored by many who think in terms of single stocks rather than a portfolio as a whole.

Part III, "Investing the Smart Way in Bonds," gives you the tools you need to invest successfully in fixed-income securities. You will learn the essentials of bonds—what they are and why they may be the best way for you to achieve a regular stream of income while protecting your assets. You will learn which bonds are the safest of all investments; which bonds will give you higher yields; how to uncover the hidden profitable opportunities that investors often overlook; which bonds pay federally tax-exempt interest; and how zero-coupon bonds can grow your capital.

Part IV, "Investing the Smart Way in Mutual Funds," explains how mutual funds work; why big investors buy mutual funds; the importance of the funds' investment objectives and policies; how the funds get paid; how you can buy funds directly and avoid sales charges; and the impact of expenses in determining a fund's performance. Several chapters are devoted to showing you how to invest the smart way in mutual funds with different objectives.

Fund shopping networks are among the newest services available to mutual fund investors. Through these one-stop sources, set up by discount brokers, you will be able to buy and sell a wide range of mutual funds, both no-load and load. The number of such sources is growing, and the practice seems destined to become a dominant way in which mutual funds are distributed.

Here are six basic rules to help you invest the smart way:

1. *Be knowledgeable.* Learn about the economy and the financial market. Evaluate carefully the objectives, strategies, management, reputation, and past performance of any investment you may consider.
2. *Be consistent.* Develop your own basic financial plan for your investment assets, and don't let anyone or anything (including the short-term fluctuations of the markets) persuade you to alter it.
3. *Be balanced.* Hold a balanced portfolio of stocks, bonds, and cash reserves as a sensible way to hedge against the future's uncertainties.
4. *Be diversified.* Whatever investment balance you select, diversify your investments among large numbers of stocks and bonds (mutual funds can help you achieve this goal nicely).
5. *Be cost conscious.* Costs reduce your return. Other things being equal, the investment program with the lowest costs (commissions, management fees, operating expenses, etc.) should provide the highest long-term return.
6. *Be skeptical.* Avoid the temptations of crowd psychology, listening to so-called pundits, and the allure of market timing. There are no easy answers in the world of investing. Accept any advice with healthy skepticism.

Finally, to invest the smart way, start *now.* The most important single factor in successful investing is time. The sooner you get started, the more time your assets will have to accumulate and the greater will be the likelihood of your building a substantial amount of wealth. Throughout the book I have provided telephone numbers (toll-free in most cases) of investment service providers and potential investment vehicles to help you in your pursuit of financial independence.

PART ONE

*A*chieving Financial Independence

CHAPTER 1

Keys to Successful Investing

*T*his chapter will help you understand some of the techniques successful investors use to achieve their investment objectives. It shows how you can develop an investment strategy and explains important investment concepts and stock market approaches.

Two widely discussed and controversial stock market theories provide an intriguing insight into the difficulty of trying to outguess the market: The random walk theory and the efficient market theory.

The Random Walk Theory

In 1900, a French mathematician named Louis Bachelier espoused the random walk theory. This theory, revived in the 1960s, holds that past prices are of no use in forecasting future price movements. Rather, stock prices reflect reactions to information coming to the market in a random way, so they are no more predictable than the walking pattern of a drunken person. Technical analysts sharply dispute this theory, saying that charts of past price movements enable them to predict future price movements.

The Efficient Market Theory

The efficient market theory also contradicts the idea of being able to predict what the market or individual stocks will do in the future. This theory says that current market prices fully reflect the knowledge and expectations of all investors. Therefore, it is futile to seek undervalued stocks or to forecast market movements. Any new development is immediately reflected in a company's stock price, making it impossible to beat the market. This loudly disputed theory also claims that an investor who throws darts at a newspaper's stock listings has as good a chance to outperform the market as any professional investor.

An interesting illustration of the dart-throwing claim was given in an experiment undertaken some years ago by NBC chief financial correspondent Mike Jensen and the late *Forbes* publisher Malcom Forbes, Jr. Forbes carefully selected five stocks, while Jensen threw five darts at an open newspaper page listing all stocks traded on the New York Stock Exchange. At the end of five years, the random group of stocks substantially outperformed Forbes' selection.

In any case, most financial analysts agree that for total return over the long term, no publicly traded investment alternative offers more potential under normal conditions than common stock. But while the historical returns are high, the volatility of the market creates risk, which is the reason for the higher returns. If you want to earn more than is available from U.S. Treasury bills (T-bills), you must assume risk.

Develop an Investment Strategy

Your investment strategy deals with the overall, long-term guidelines you set up in an attempt to ensure success in meeting your financial goals. Tactics are used to implement a strategy and relate to activities of shorter duration. This chapter focuses on strategy, which crafts the lifetime decisions you make in the course of managing your investment portfolio.

Two basic requirements are involved in long-term planning and decision making:

1. You must have a clearly defined objective.
2. You must have a specific time horizon.

For most investors, investing goes through two general stages:

1. The *accumulation stage,* when your earnings exceed your expenses, and you are building wealth

2. The *withdrawal stage,* which begins when you start consuming your accumulated wealth

Following are key points to remember when developing a long-term investment strategy:

*   *When developing a long-term investment strategy, think in terms of a time horizon of at least five years.* Only assets that you will not need for at least five years should be committed to your program.
*   *Do not invest all your assets in common stocks.* Unexpected events may require that you dip into savings, even while you still are accumulating wealth. Taking money out of the stock market at the wrong time can seriously hurt your long-term strategy. So keep enough liquid assets available for the inevitable emergencies life throws at you.

Investment Concepts

To develop a successful long-term investment strategy, you need to understand how your strategy fits in with current stock market investment research and theory.

Managing Risk

Think of *risk* as the possibility that your investment will be worth less at the end of your holding period than it was at the time of your original purchase. Inflation can be taken into account by saying that risk is the possibility that your investment will be worth less in "real dollars" (adjusted for inflation) at the end of the holding period. Another way to approach risk is to say that risk is the possibility that your investment will be worth less than if you had put it into a zero-risk investment, such as a money-market fund or T-bill.

Many investors use statistics to provide a measurable definition of risk. This definition measures variability, the amount by which your investment return could vary around the expected average return. For example, suppose a five-year certificate of deposit has a guaranteed 6 percent return over the holding period. Because the 6 percent return is guaranteed, there is no other possible realized return and therefore no variability—the risk is zero.

Now, suppose you are presented with a second potential investment that has a 50 percent chance of a 40 percent return and a 50 percent chance of a 10 percent loss over the holding period. The mathematically expected return on this second investment is 15 percent [(50%×40%)+(50%×−10%)]. But the actual return may be different from the expected return of 15 percent. We see here the existence of risk. The greater the potential variability, the greater the risk.

Potential variability can be used to compare the riskiness of different investments and to make judgments about the suitability of a particular investment for your portfolio, taking into consideration your own level of comfort for risk. In practical terms, you often will determine the riskiness of a particular investment subjectively, using research and other information that is available to you.

However, comparing the 6 percent guaranteed investment with no risk to the second investment with an expected return of 15 percent, but having some risk, we are not able to say which is the better investment. Higher return means higher risk. The investment choice depends on the trade-off between risk and return that you are willing to make. Your objectives should be considered in terms of both reward and risk. In an efficient market, expected returns will be higher for securities that have higher degrees of risk.

How long you hold your securities has an important impact on the risk and return trade-off. For example, the risk and return trade-off for a one-year holding period will be different from the trade-off for a five-year holding period. Stock market risk tends to decline as the holding period lengthens. Therefore, setting a proper time frame is very important when making investment decisions.

Reducing Risk through Diversification

In the stock and bond markets, two factors can cause a stock's return to vary. One relates to changes in the corporation or the way investors perceive the company. The other has to do with movements in the overall securities markets. This means there are two components to the risk that an investor faces:

1. *Market risk,* which is inherent in the market itself
2. *Company risk,* which has to do with the unique characteristics of any one stock or bond and the industry in which it operates

About 70 percent of the risk you face as an investor is company risk. Fortunately, you can eliminate this risk by diversifying among different securities. For example, you can invest in ten different stocks or bonds rather than just one.

Market risk is the other 30 percent of total risk and cannot be avoided by diversification, for all stocks and bonds are affected to some degree by the overall market.

The fact that you can eliminate company risk simply by diversifying your portfolio is critical to the long-term success of your investment strategy. An investor who owns just one stock is taking on 100 percent of the risk associated with investing in common stocks, while an investor with a diversified portfolio has only 30 percent of that risk. Put differently, a single-stock investor has more than three times the risk of a diversified investor.

Investors who think of themselves as conservative but who invest in one low-risk stock actually incur more risk than investors who have a portfolio of ten aggressive growth stocks. In addition, the conservative investors are getting a lower expected return, for they are invested in lower-risk, lower-return stocks.

This brings us to an important investment concept. The stock and bond markets provide higher returns for higher risks, but they provide those higher returns only for *unavoidable risk.* Company risk is mostly avoidable through diversification. Regardless of what investment objective you may have, what your intended holding period is, or what kind of securities analysis is performed, *if you do not have a diversified portfolio, you are either throwing away return or assuming risk that could be avoided (or dramatically reduced), or both.*

For adequate diversification, your portfolio should contain at least ten different stocks or bonds, with approximately equal dollar amounts in each. In buying stocks, select companies that appear to offer the greatest chance for future earnings expansion.

Invest the Smart Way

*R*emember, the volatility of financial markets creates risk. Risk is the reason you have the potential to earn more than is available from T-bills, but you must develop an investment strategy. It should deal with the overall, long-term guidelines you set up in an attempt to ensure success in meeting your financial goals.

CHAPTER 2

Creating Your Own Financial Plan

*A*chieving financial independence requires a disciplined, systematic approach to investing. You need to know whether you have the right mix of investments for your personal situation. Today investors can choose from more than 6,000 stocks and bonds, and more than more than 7,500 mutual funds. This chapter will help you form your own investment objectives, sort through the huge number of offerings, and develop a well-designed plan for investing.

Long-Term Focus

The long-term focus of your financial plan considers commitments made for five years or more. For example, many investors set retirement and college funding as their high-priority objectives.

Saving, where safety and conservatism are important, differs from *investing,* which involves taking a certain degree of risk with your money in pursuit of higher returns. Investment programs involving stocks, bonds, and mutual funds have delivered higher returns over time than FDIC-insured savings accounts and T-bills, but they also decline in value from time to time, and are not FDIC-insured.

If you cannot tolerate fluctuating values in your assets, you probably should avoid the securities markets. This book is designed for investors who can patiently wait out short-term declines in the stock and bond markets as they pursue potentially higher long-term returns.

Short-Term Needs

Construct your long-term investment program on a savings foundation that holds sufficient funds for short-term needs. Short-term monies are those that you may need within five years. Goals may include a "rainy day" fund for emergencies or savings for a car, vacation, home, or other purpose. Financial planners typically recommend an emergency fund of about six months' worth of living expenses. As much as a year's worth might be appropriate for someone who is self-employed or retired. You can add to that the total of other short-term goals you may have.

Your short-term savings should be accessible and safe. Popular choices for many investors include money-market funds, bank certificates of deposit (CDs), T-bills, and short-term bond funds. Bank CDs pay a fixed rate of interest and the principal is guaranteed by an agency of the U.S. government, but you may be subject to a penalty for early withdrawal. Money-market fund yields fluctuate and lack a government guarantee, but are quickly available and offer competitive market returns. Treasury bills pay a fixed rate of interest and are guaranteed by the U.S. government. Short-term bond funds may pay a little higher return and are an option for investors willing to take a small amount of risk.

Classes of Assets

The most critical step in creating a long-term investment program is to allocate your assets by striking a balance among the three common investment classes:

1. *Cash reserve securities* provide stable investment value and current investment income. This group includes money-market funds, T-bills, and bank CDs.
2. *Bonds* are interest-bearing obligations issued by corporations; the federal government and its agencies; and state and local governments. The yields offered by these securities are generally higher than those of cash reserves, but their value fluctuates with bond market conditions.

3. *Common stocks* represent ownership rights in a corporation. They usually pay dividends and offer potential for capital growth. Stock market risk can be substantial, however.

Your future investment returns depend to a great extent on how you allocate your money among these three classes.

Risk and Return: Discovering the Trade-Off

Common stocks have historically delivered the highest average annual returns of the three investment classes. According to Ibbotson Associates, the average annual return on stocks between 1926 and 1996, was 10.5 percent. Bonds had an average return of 5.2 percent, and the average return on cash reserves was 3.7 percent. These percentages represent total return: income or yield plus any capital gain or loss.

Since 1965, a $10,000 investment in T-bills would have grown to $70,360, in long-term government bonds to $98,340, and in common stocks (S&P 500) to $210,140. Over the past 30 years, an investment in stocks would have grown to more than twice the value of the same investment in bonds or cash reserves.

While stocks and bonds may offer higher returns than cash reserves, they also expose you to more risk. This is a trade-off: To pursue higher investment returns, you must be willing to assume higher risk.

Inflation risk—the risk that the general increase in the cost of living (inflation) will reduce the real value of your investment—is also important to keep in mind. If the total return on your investment is 10 percent, but inflation is 4 percent, your actual or "real" return is only 6 percent. For more about risk, refer back to Chapter 1.

Allocating Your Assets— Striking the Right Balance for You

How you divide your savings among cash reserves, bonds, and stocks depends on four factors:

1. Your financial situation
2. Your objectives
3. Your time horizon
4. Your ability to tolerate risk

Of these, perhaps the most important factor is time. The longer you have to invest, the greater the risk you can assume.

Investing for Retirement

If you are investing for retirement, your objective during your working years is to accumulate assets. Your investment plan should emphasize growth. With retirement investing, you have the time to take measured risks. While you are in your 20s, 30s, and even 40s, you have a time horizon extending for decades.

After you retire, your objectives include preserving the money that has built up and spending it to support your lifestyle. At that time your investments should emphasize income, with some growth of capital to offset inflation. With today's longer life expectancies, you could still be investing for 20 or 30 years after retirement. These long spans provide the time to ride out short-term market fluctuations.

With these objectives in mind, your asset allocation for retirement should emphasize stocks when you are young and bonds and cash reserves as you grow older. Of course, always keep separate savings reserved for emergencies and short-term objectives.

Investing for Your Children's Education

In some ways, investing for college is similar to investing for retirement. When your child is young, your objective is to achieve maximum growth of your capital. Then, when your child enters college, you need ready access to your money as various bills come due. At the same time, your education fund should continue to earn a reasonable return.

Of course, an education plan has a different, shorter time frame than a retirement plan does. If your child begins college at age 18 for an undergraduate degree, the time is about 22 years. Once your child enters the teenage years, little time is left to recoup possible investment losses that may occur. The shorter the time left until college entry, the less risk you should take with your investments.

As in retirement planning, your asset allocation for college investments should emphasize stocks during the early years, when your child is young, then turn more conservative when your child enters the teen years. In the final span, your college investments should consist mainly of money-market instruments and short-term bonds.

Allocating Assets at Different Age Levels

By diversifying your portfolio of securities, you can pretty easily strike a good investment balance to fulfill your objectives. Figure 2.1 suggests an asset allocation program to meet the needs of investors at different age levels.

If you are 20 to 50 years old, having a growth objective to build your retirement fund is appropriate. When you near retirement, from age 51 to age 60, move to a balanced growth approach to reduce the risk of large losses. Then in early retirement, spread some assets into cash reserves to protect capital even more while maintaining conservative growth. During your later years, you will have more concern for current income than growth, so you can transfer more funds from stocks to bonds.

Which Types of Investments Should You Choose?

Once you've decided how to allocate your assets to meet your long-term objectives, the next step is to select specific investments. Consider a number of important issues in planning your investment portfolio. (Other chapters in this book cover each issue in some detail.) Following are the main aspects you should consider in your decision.

Stocks

Stocks are generally divided into *growth stocks* and *value stocks*. You can purchase growth stocks when your objective is capital gains; buy value stocks when you want dividend income. Growth stocks are recommended for portfolios where growth and balanced growth are the major objectives. Value stocks appeal more to older or more conservative investors whose portfolios are geared to conservative growth and income. Many stocks are further subdivided into such groups as aggressive growth, growth and income, income, and small company.

Bonds

Bonds vary according to risk and duration. In choosing a bond, consider the following questions:

- How much risk are you willing to assume? In general, the higher the income yield a bond pays, the greater the risk.

FIGURE 2.1   Allocating Assets at Different Age Levels

Objective	Your Age	Allocation	Historic Returns*
Growth	20–50	80% Stocks 20% Bonds	+9.8%
Balanced Growth	51–60	60% Stocks 40% Bonds	+8.9%
Conservative Growth	61–75	40% Stocks 40% Bonds 20% Cash Reserves	+7.6%
Income	76+	20% Stocks 60% Bonds 20% Cash Reserves	+6.3%

*Average returns for 1926–1995.

- Should you investigate the benefits of tax-exempt versus taxable bonds? Top tax bracket investors can receive income that is exempt from both federal and state taxes.

Other Stocks and Bonds

- *International stocks and bonds* can provide additional diversification, but are subject to currency fluctuations and other risks.
- *Small company stocks* have the potential for higher returns, but entail greater risk from stock market volatility.
- *Specific industry stocks* can offer possibly higher returns from high-growth areas such as biotechnology or computers.
- *Junk bonds* produce higher yields, but at significantly greater risk because of their lower credit quality.

Designing Your Investment Strategy

Timing Your Investments

Some investors pursue a strategy of attempting to "time" the market. This involves moving in and out of stocks and bonds, hoping to buy when prices are low and sell when prices are high, with a goal of avoiding market declines. Unfortunately, few investors (if any) can accurately foresee the direction of the stock or bond markets.

Dollar Cost Averaging

This strategy avoids the pitfalls of market timing. Under a dollar cost averaging program, you invest a certain dollar amount on a regular schedule, regardless of market conditions. If you are investing in mutual funds, the plan can be implemented by using electronic transfers from your checking account to your fund, by automatic transfers from a money-market fund, through payroll deduction in an employer-sponsored retirement plan, or by simply mailing a check each month to your fund.

As Chapter 3 will show, dollar cost averaging can be critical to your achieving long-term investment success.

Common Mistakes to Avoid

Try to avoid these four common mistakes whether you are investing in stocks, bonds, or mutual funds:

1. *Buying the most recent best performer.* In any market environment, some stocks and mutual funds have produced phenomenal returns. Unfortunately, too often last year's best performers become this year's laggards. Special market conditions can make particular stocks act like shooting stars—but like these, they can fade as suddenly as they appeared. In the same way, aggressive or specialty techniques can rocket a fund to the top one year, then lead it to a dizzying decline the next. Stocks and mutual funds that consistently perform well year in and year out, tend to end up in the top 10 percent over a decade or longer.

2. *Acting on intuition and hunches.* Few people are able to accurately forecast market trends. You will be better off developing a consistent, disciplined approach to investing and sticking to it. Successful investors who endure practice discipline and consistency.

3. *Overdiversifying.* Diversification is a primary attribute of successful investing. But purchase and sale commissions make it costly for an investor of limited means to buy only a few shares of dozens of stocks. Often it makes more sense to buy a mutual fund and obtain instant cost-effective diversification. In the same way, investors who own dozens of mutual funds (which as a whole behave like the market) can save themselves a lot of trouble by buying a low-cost index fund. (For more on index funds, see Chapter 35.)

4. *Selling too soon.* Investment styles tend to go in and out of favor. During some years the market will favor growth stocks, small company stocks, or undervalued stocks. When a style goes out of favor for several years, stock performance in that group will suffer, but those stocks will also rebound when the style returns to favor. The danger you face as an investor is selling a stock or fund right before its performance improves in favor of a security whose performance is about to weaken.

Other Considerations

Always know the *costs* of investing in a potential security or mutual fund. Because costs necessarily reduce investment returns, lower costs inevitably mean higher returns.

Consider *taxes* in your investment planning. Investing in a tax-deferred individual retirement account (IRA) or company-sponsored 401(k) plan can have an important long-term effect on your investment return. Also consider the taxability of income and capital gain distributions, as well as the tax effect of going in and out of securities investments. (For more on tax implications, see Chapter 5.)

If you are evaluating a mutual fund, one factor to consider is its *past performance.* Remember, though, the caveat that applies to every mutual fund: Past performance is not necessarily an indication of future income or total return.

Invest the Smart Way

Your goal of financial independence requires a disciplined, systematic approach to investing. Maintain a long-term focus, making commitments intended for five years or more.

CHAPTER 3

The All-Time Favorite Investment Technique

*F*ew investment techniques have so well stood the test of time that one can confidently say, "This works." But such a method exists. It is easy, it works, and you can do it. Called *dollar cost averaging,* this plan is simply the practice of buying securities at regular intervals in fixed dollar amounts, regardless of price levels.

Small investors have amassed fortunes by making systematic purchases of shares over long periods. For instance, by putting aside as little as $50 each month in mutual funds, you can take advantage of dollar cost averaging, one of the simplest and most effective ways of building an investment portfolio. Larger investment amounts usually are needed to purchase individual stocks and bonds, but the principle is the same.

When you follow this procedure, you purchase more shares at relatively low prices than at high prices. As a result, the average *cost* of all shares bought turns out to be lower than the average of all the *prices* at which purchases were made. The combination of buying shares at a variety of price levels and acquiring more shares at low rather than high prices has proven to be an efficient and cost-effective method of accumulating securities.

Average Cost versus Average Price

The arithmetic that illustrates how dollar cost averaging works is simple. You need only remember that by periodically purchasing shares with identical amounts of money, as long as share prices change at all during the investment period, the average cost of shares purchased will be less than the average of the prices paid. For example, say that you decide to invest $280 regularly. You make five purchases totaling $1,400 at prices between $10 and $5 a share. The number of shares bought for each $280 purchase in this example would be as follows (transaction costs are not considered):

Price	Shares Purchased
$10	28
8	35
7	40
5	56
8	35

Total shares acquired for $1,400 investment: 194
Average cost of each share ($1,400 divided by 194): $7.22
Average price of shares purchased: $7.60

This program works because an *equal number of dollars buys more shares at low prices than at high prices.* It is essential that you make purchases at low prices when they are available. If you consider dollar cost averaging, you must take into account your emotional and financial ability to continue making new investments through periods of low price levels.

Dollar cost averaging does not guarantee that you will always have profits in your portfolio or that you will never incur losses. Use an investment program like this only for long-term purposes. You should be pretty sure that you will not need these invested funds for several years.

Dollar cost averaging can substantially reduce the risks inherent in securities investing. Shares are bound to be purchased over the years at a variety of price levels—high, low, and in-between. That fact alone should provide better income and capital gains than haphazard investing or buying only when the outlook appears bright.

Growth Is Not Essential

Fluctuating security prices are more important to successful dollar cost averaging than long-term growth alone. This surprising fact arises because you get your best opportunity to acquire a large number of shares during periods of declining prices.

Continuing the previous example, assume that after you make the five purchases, the share price returns to $10, the level of the first purchase. The 194 shares you already own have a value of $1,940. Your profit is $560. (During the purchase period, we assume that the price had declined as much as 50 percent.)

Now, instead of a drop in price, let's see what happens if the share price had steadily advanced to an increase of 50 percent and the five equal purchases of $280 were made, again until the full $1,400 was invested. For this example, let's assume that you purchase fractional shares, as is the case with mutual funds:

Price	Shares Purchased
$10	28.00
11	25.45
12	23.33
14	20.00
15	18.67

Total shares acquired for $1,400 investment: 115.45
Average cost of each share ($1,400 divided by 115.45): $12.13
Average price of shares purchased: $12.40

In this example, the process of dollar cost averaging also results in an average cost that is less than the average price. But notice that after a 50 percent increase from the initial price of $10 per share, the total value of the 115.45 shares at $15 is $1,731.75. Although still a profit, the result is about 10.7 percent less than the $1,940 that the 194 shares in the previous example were worth at $10.

Of course, investors have no control over the direction security prices will take once they start a dollar cost averaging program. The plan's main advantage is that in the long run it will work to your benefit almost regardless of what the market does. This is particularly important if you are among those investors who fear starting an investment plan because you believe stock prices are too high. If you are correct and the market does decline, the timing may be just right to begin dollar cost averaging.

Reinvesting Dividends

Many investors who invest in securities on a periodic basis can and do reinvest any dividends they receive. The effect in the beginning is minor, but as the program continues, the impact of compounding shares becomes more and more significant. The relative importance will vary, of course, depending on the emphasis that a particular company or fund places on paying income distributions on its shares.

As mentioned earlier, building a fortune by investing in stocks, bonds, or mutual funds is less a matter of investment skill or luck than of persistence and patience. The first decision to make is whether you truly are willing to forgo immediate gratification to achieve a long-term investment goal. Because the goal is to invest a fixed amount of money on a regular basis for many years, ask yourself the question: "Do I want a Mercedes today, or a fortune tomorrow?"

An Example of Dollar Cost Averaging

Many fine investments are available among stocks, bonds, and mutual funds. This book highlights a few. Now I'll show you how dollar cost averaging would have worked for an investor who started such a program at age 35 and continued it until retirement at age 65, making investments of $5,000 at the beginning of each year from 1967 to 1996 in Mutual Shares Fund. This fund has had a good record through the years, although other funds and stock investments have done even better. There were several years when the fund's shares declined in value, but patient investors have been well rewarded.

If you had invested $5,000 in Mutual Shares Fund at the beginning of 1967 and then regularly added $5,000 each year for a total of $150,000, you would have amassed more than $5 million by the end of 1996. (See Figure 3.1.) Assume that income and capital gains distributions were automatically reinvested. No provision has been made for income taxes.

FIGURE 3.1   Results of $5,000 Invested in Mutual Shares Fund on
January 2, 1966, plus $5,000 at the beginning of each
Year to December 31, 1996

End of Year	Total Return	Amount Invested	Value of Shares	Accumulated Amount Invested
1967	32.22%	$5,000	$ 7,933	$ 5,000
1968	39.97	5,000	18,102	10,000
1969	−19.21	5,000	18,664	15,000
1970	−8.98	5,000	21,539	20,000
1971	22.28	5,000	32,452	25,000
1972	.53	5,000	37,650	30,000
1973	−8.11	5,000	39,191	35,000
1974	8.16	5,000	47,798	40,000
1975	34.12	5,000	70,812	45,000
1976	55.21	5,000	117,667	50,000
1977	15.61	5,000	141,816	55,000
1978	18.11	5,000	173,405	60,000
1979	42.69	5,000	254,566	65,000
1980	19.38	5,000	309,870	70,000
1981	8.93	5,000	342,988	75,000
1982	12.87	5,000	392,774	80,000
1983	36.64	5,000	543,517	85,000
1984	14.47	5,000	627,887	90,000
1985	26.73	5,000	802,058	95,000
1986	16.99	5,000	944,177	100,000
1987	6.34	5,000	1,009,355	105,000
1988	30.69	5,000	1,325,661	110,000
1989	14.93	5,000	1,529,328	115,000
1990	−9.82	5,000	1,379,148	120,000
1991	20.99	5,000	1,674,681	125,000
1992	21.33	5,000	2,036,890	130,000
1993	20.99	5,000	2,469,434	135,000
1994	4.55	5,000	3,598,026	140,000
1995	29.10	5,000	4,650,051	145,000
1996	20.80	5,000	5,622,262	150,000

Beginning a Dollar Cost Averaging Program before a Downturn

If, however, you had started the plan in Figure 3.1 with a $5,000 investment on January 2, 1969 (after the fund had enjoyed two very good years), the account would have shown a substantial loss at the end of both 1969 and 1970. In 1969, the fund suffered a loss per share of 19.21 percent and a loss of 8.98 percent in 1970. At the end of 1969, with $5,000 invested, the account value would have been $4,040, and at the end of 1970, with $10,000 invested, the value would have been $8,228.

By persevering, however, you would have benefited by buying more shares at the lower prices. In 1971, the fund rebounded with a gain of 22.28 percent, then had mixed results for the next three years. But in 1975, the fund gained 34.12 percent and then 55.21 percent in 1976. By the end of 1976, with $40,000 invested, you would have had a value of $83,813.

During this erratic eight-year span, with substantial losses in three years and one flat year, if you had stuck with the program, you would have ended up with a very nice profit. More important, by not losing heart during the down years, the portfolio was set to take advantage of the next 17 years, during which only 1990 had a negative return.

A no-load fund until 1996, Mutual Shares Fund was acquired by the Franklin Templeton group and is now sold with a sales charge. You can get a prospectus and complete information on Mutual Shares Fund by calling 800-342-5236.

Invest the Smart Way

Small investors have amassed fortunes by making systematic purchases of shares over long periods. You can too, by investing a fixed number of dollars on a regular basis regardless of price levels.

CHAPTER 4

How to Minimize Brokerage Costs

*A*ttorneys' ads are often followed by a caveat such as "The hiring of an attorney is an important decision that should not be based solely upon advertisements." This is sound advice and applies to many other choices we make—including the selection of a securities broker. In choosing your broker, think in terms of *cost-effectiveness.* Consider what services you need from a broker, which broker—or type of broker—can best serve your needs, and finally, which broker can provide the services you need at the least cost.

Securities brokers generally provide a variety of services for their customers, enabling customers to buy and sell stocks, bonds, mutual funds, commodities, options, limited partnerships, certificates of deposit, annuities, and other financial products. In addition, brokers may offer asset management accounts that combine a customer's holdings of stocks and bonds with money-market funds. The customer can then write checks against the account, which may also have credit-card features. Brokers can send you annual reports on the companies whose securities you are considering. These reports contain financial statements reflecting a company's assets, liabilities, and income reports. Many brokers also offer individualized financial planning services. With the wide choice of products and services they have made available to the public, brokers today have a wide-ranging clientele, from novice investors to wealthy and sophisticated individuals and institutions.

Full-Service versus Discount Brokers

Prior to 1975, all brokers charged the same fixed commission rates. On May 1, 1975, known as May Day in the brokerage industry, the era of fixed commissions ended. Since then, brokers have been free to charge whatever they like. The resulting greater competition within the industry introduced the public to a new type of broker: the *discounter.* These brokers specialize in executing orders to buy and sell stocks, bonds, options, and mutual funds. Usually, they charge commissions that are far less than full-service brokers, but they also offer fewer services.

Discount brokers account for about 25 percent of all brokerage trades of stocks and earn roughly 15 percent of commission dollars. They come in three types:

1. The "Big Three" are Charles Schwab, Fidelity Brokerage, and Quick & Reilly. Together they earn about 70 percent of the discount brokerage revenue.
2. Banks, most of which operate locally, account for 10 percent of the discount business.
3. The balance goes to *deep-discount* brokers.

On average, the Big Three charge 58 percent less than the commissions charged by full-service brokers, such as Merrill Lynch, Pierce, Fenner & Smith (the largest broker in terms of number of account executives). According to Mercer, Inc., a New York research firm, the 30 deepest discounters charge 78 percent less than the rates typical of full-service brokers. The Big Three and banks usually charge by a transaction's dollar value, determined by multiplying the number of shares times the market price. Deep-discount brokers charge by the number of shares traded in the transaction. Some brokers offer both approaches. Nearly all brokers have a minimum transaction fee.

Full-service brokers offer investors far more guidance on what investments are appropriate for each client. Clients pay substantially higher charges for this guidance. Full-service brokers may also engage in investment banking, helping raise capital for federal, state, and local governments and for corporations. This involves underwriting new issues of stocks and bonds for corporations, as well as debt issues for governments, and distributing them to both institutional and individual investors.

If you are doing business with a full-service broker, be particularly careful about which account executive deals with you. Brokerage firm employees are paid on the basis of the amount of commissions they develop from customers. As a result, they are under constant pressure to produce. This pressure to produce commissions often leads to various abuses.

One abuse to watch for is the recommendation of an investment that is unsuitable for you, but may be appropriate for a speculator with a high tolerance for risk. So-called *penny stocks* or other very volatile securities might be recommended if the broker believes you are looking for something that will quickly increase in price. Or, if you are seeking income, a risky *junk bond* might be suggested. Another abuse employed by a hungry broker is *churning,* excessive trading of a client's account. Churning increases a broker's commissions but usually leaves you worse off, or no better off, than before the activity occurred. Churning is illegal under Securities and Exchange Commission (SEC) and stock exchange rules, but is difficult to prove. Clients who believe they are victims of churning or are being sold inappropriate investments can sue or take their complaint to arbitration.

If you are going to deal with a full-service brokerage firm, ask for a mature person who has been in the business for at least five years. After you have been assigned a broker, sit down together to discuss your financial situation and investment objectives. Be sure your broker knows how much risk you are willing to take. Being comfortable with your broker is important.

If you require less hand-holding, a discount broker may serve you just as well and at much less cost. In many cases discounters offer more services than you might expect. Their objective is to offer an investing climate that is easy, convenient, and inexpensive, plus a certain amount of the help you need to make informed decisions. In dealing with a discount broker, expect to pay less in commissions and account fees. The Big Three firms offer free investment guides and even seminars. Plus, you have a wide range of different investments to choose from, such as the following:

- *Stocks:* both listed and over the counter
- *Mutual funds:* both load and no-load
- *Government securities:* U.S. Treasury bills, notes, and bonds
- *Fixed-income investments:* municipal bonds, corporate bonds, government agency securities, and other fixed-income investments

FIGURE 4.1   Sample Commissions for Buying or Selling Stocks

	100 Shares @ $10.00	500 Shares @ $15.00	1,000 Shares @ $20.00
Fidelity	$46.50	$101.00	$143.50
Merrill Lynch	50.00	174.00	374.00
Quick & Reilly	37.50	77.75	109.00
Charles Schwab	47.00	101.50	144.00
Smith Barney	50.00	150.00	400.00
Vanguard	41.00	80.00	120.00

Comparing Commissions

You will find substantial differences in transaction charges made by full-service brokers, large discount brokers, and deep-discount brokers. But pricing in the industry can be complex. In addition to minimum fees, some brokers charge for postage, stock transfers, and inactive accounts. Certain brokers offer discounts for electronically placed orders and rebates for monthly trading that exceeds a stated minimum. Figure 4.1 lists the results of a January 1997 telephone survey of several brokers. It indicates the commissions you would be charged if you bought shares in various amounts and at different price levels. Remember, commissions and fees are always subject to change. Ask your broker for a current commission schedule.

Like those at full-service brokers, customers' securities accounts at discount brokers are insured for at least $500,000 by the Securities Investor Protection Corporation (SIPC), a nonprofit company established by Congress.

To give you an idea of what commissions you would expect to pay a typical discount broker for stock transactions, Figure 4.2 shows the Vanguard Discount Brokerage Services commission schedule in effect at the writing of this book.

Some discount brokers permit you to trade directly via a telephone or by using your personal computer. AccuTrade, for instance, allows you to enter orders 24 hours a day; view your positions, balances, and open orders; and receive stock quotes 24 hours a day. They charge 3 cents per share traded, regardless of stock price, with a $48 minimum commission. Charles Schwab & Company offers online trading with similar features, using their software or the Web. Their basic charge is $29.95 per trade up to 1,000 shares. Wherever you deal, always be sure to ask what other charges may be applicable.

FIGURE 4.2   Vanguard Discount Brokerage Services Commission
Schedule

Commission Schedule

A separate commission is charged for each security purchased or
sold; the commission schedule is subject to change.

Stocks

Principal	multiplied by	Factor	plus	Base
$0 to $2,500	×	0.016	+	$ 25
$2,501 to $5,000	×	0.0084	+	$ 35
$5,001 to $15,000	×	0.004	+	$ 50
$15,001 to $50,000	×	0.003	+	$ 60
$50,001 to $250,000	×	0.00125	+	$100
$250,001 and Over	×	0.0011	+	$125*

Minimum Commission: $36.25 or $.0275 per share, whichever is greater
Maximum Commission: $.48 per share

*Negotiable

Stocks Priced Less Than $1.00

$36.25 + 3% of principal

Corporate/Municipal/Zero Coupon/ Government Agency Bonds

$35 Minimum
$1,000 Face Amount = 1 Bond

1st to 24th Bond	$25 + $3 per bond
Each Additional Bond	$2 per bond

Treasury Securities

There is a $35 flat fee for Treasuries purchased at the auction.
Treasuries purchased on the secondary market should follow the
corporate bond schedule up to a maximum of $50.

There is a 5-bond minimum on Treasury zeros and a 25-bond
minimum on GNMAs.

Options

Principal	multiplied by	Factor	plus	Base
Under $3,000	×	0.012	+	$25
$3,001 to $10,000	×	0.009	+	$25
$10,001 and Over	×	0.006	+	$25

The minimum commission for an option transaction is $2.50 per
contract or $35, whichever is greater. This minimum charge applies
to all options transactions regardless of the contract price.

It is almost impossible to determine who is the cheapest broker. The answer depends on the size and type of trade involved. To select the best broker for you, first determine what your average transaction size will be, then shop around.

Fortunately, some researchers have already done the shopping for you. For a nominal fee, the American Association of Individual Investors (312-280-0170) annually produces a report that calculates the fees for three typical trades—100 shares at $50, 500 shares at $50, and 1,000 shares at $5—charged by about 70 nonbank discount brokers. For a little higher cost, Mercer, Inc., provides much more detailed information in their *Discount Broker Survey,* which features fees most industry brokers charge for 22 different trades (800-582-9854).

A discount broker is likely near you. The yellow page section of your phone book lists all the discount brokers, as well as full-service brokers, in your area under "Stock and Bond Brokers."

Invest the Smart Way

*T*o increase the return on your investments, minimize brokerage costs. In choosing a broker, determine the services you need and how much you are willing to pay. Generally, the less you pay, the fewer services you should expect to receive.

CHAPTER 5

How Taxes Affect Your Investment Returns

*T*axation is a price you pay for successful investing. Investors typically concentrate on achieving maximum *pretax* returns. But, what matters most is what's left for you *after* taxes. Investing in stocks, bonds, and mutual funds has many advantages, but beware of a potential hazard: The turnover of securities within your own or a mutual fund's portfolio often causes the realization of *capital gains,* the profits realized when the net cost of securities purchased is deducted from the net sales proceeds. A mutual fund must pass on these gains to all shareholders as taxable distributions, regardless of each investor's tax situation. For many investors, higher marginal federal income tax brackets as well as many states' taxes affect taxable dividends.

Let's look at an example of how both pretax and after-tax returns can work in two actual mutual funds over ten years. The following chart shows the effects of a $10,000 investment made in each of two common stock funds in June 1984. Before considering taxes, the Vanguard Windsor Fund produced a significantly higher return than the Neuberger & Berman Manhattan Fund. But on an after-tax basis, assuming tax rates of 36 percent on ordinary income and 28 percent on capital gains, the net proceeds from the Neuberger & Berman fund were greater.

| | Value of Investment | |
	Before Taxes	After Taxes
Neuberger & Berman Manhattan Fund	$39,300	$29,700
Vanguard Windsor Fund	43,400	28,700

To help you develop a tax-efficient investment strategy, this chapter describes the impact of federal taxes on income and capital gains under the provisions of current tax law and provides guidance on ways in which you can minimize your portfolio's exposure to taxes.

Taxation of Interest and Dividend Income

Publicly held corporations will tell you whether their distributions are taxable. Taxable dividends paid to you are reported to the Internal Revenue Service (IRS) by the paying company on Form 1099-DIV, a copy of which is sent to you. Taxable interest paid to you is reported to the IRS by the payer on Form 1099-INT. The IRS uses this information as a check on your reporting of dividends and interest.

Cash dividends.   Cash dividends you receive that are paid out of current or accumulated earnings of a corporation are subject to tax as ordinary income.

Dividends reinvested in company stock.   Some companies allow you to take dividends in cash or to reinvest the dividends in company stock. If you elect the stock plan and pay fair market value for the stock, the full cash dividend is taxable.

If the plan allows you to buy the stock at a discounted price, the amount of the taxable dividend is the fair market value of the stock on the dividend payment date, less any service fee charged for the acquisition.

Stock dividends and stock splits.   If you own common stock and receive additional shares of the same company as a dividend, the dividend is generally not taxed. A stock dividend is taxed if you choose to receive cash instead of stock or if the stock is that of another corporation. Preferred shareholders are generally taxed on stock dividends.

Stock splits resemble the receipt of stock dividends, but they are not dividends. If you receive additional shares as part of a stock split, the new shares are not taxable. Even though you own more shares, your ownership percentage in the company has not changed.

Investment publications such as Moody's or Standard & Poor's annual dividend record books, available at many public libraries, provide details of dividend distributions and their tax treatment.

Real estate investment trust (REIT) dividends.   Ordinary dividends from an REIT are fully taxable. Dividends designated by the trust as capital gain distributions are reported as long-term capital gains regardless of how long you have held your trust shares.

Return of capital distributions.   A distribution that is not paid out of earnings is a nontaxable return of capital. It is, in effect, a partial payback of your investment. The distribution will be reported by the company on Form 1099-DIV as a nontaxable distribution.

Nontaxable distributions result in a reduction of the cost basis of your investment. If a return of capital distribution reduces your basis to zero, any further distributions are taxable as capital gains.

Money-market fund distributions.   Distributions paid to you by money-market funds are reportable as dividends. Do not confuse these with bank money-market accounts, which pay interest, not dividends.

Interest on corporate bonds.   Interest is taxable when you receive it or it is made available to you.

Interest on U.S. Treasury obligations.   Interest on securities issued by the federal government is fully taxable on your federal return. However, interest on federal obligations is not subject to state or local income taxes. Interest on bonds and notes is taxable in the year received.

On a T-bill held to maturity, you report as interest the difference between the discounted price you paid and the amount you receive on redeeming the bill at maturity. If you dispose of the bill prior to maturity, taxable interest is the difference between the discounted price you paid and the proceeds you received.

Market discount on bonds.   When the price of a bond declines because its interest rate is less than the current interest rate, a market discount occurs. Gain on a disposition of a bond bought after April 30, 1993, is taxable as ordinary income to the extent of the accrued market discount, unless you reported it annually as interest income.

Original issue discount (OID) on bonds.   OID occurs when a bond is issued for a price less than its face or principal amount and is the difference between the principal amount and the issue price. All obligations that pay no interest before maturity, such as zero-coupon bonds, are considered to be issued at a discount. Normally, a portion of the OID must be reported as interest income each year you hold the bond.

Interest on state and local government obligations.

Normally, you pay no federal tax on interest on bonds or notes of states, cities, counties, the District of Columbia, or a possession of the United States. However, interest on certain state and city obligations is taxable, such as federally guaranteed obligations and private activity bonds.

Most states tax the municipal bonds of other states, but not their own. A few states and the District of Columbia do not tax the interest on any municipal obligations.

Taxation of Capital Gains and Losses

Net capital gains (capital gains less capital losses) are added to your other income and are subject to capital gains tax rates. If your top rate is 15 percent, the capital gains are taxed at 10 percent. If your top rate is 28 percent or higher, net long-term gains in excess of short-term losses are subject to a top rate of 20 percent. Capital losses are deductible from capital gains and are deductible from as much as $3,000 of ordinary income, with a carryover for the excess over $3,000. The holding period to qualify for capital gains treatment is 18 months. Short-term gains (on assets held less than 18 months) are taxed according to your regular tax bracket.

The taxable gain or loss realized from the sale of a security is calculated by deducting your cost from your net sales proceeds. Purchase expenses, such as commissions, are included in your cost. Beginning in 2001, a new top rate of 18 percent takes effect for assets purchased after 2000 and held at least five years.

Figuring the holding period.

The holding period for stocks purchased on a public exchange starts on the day after your purchase order is executed. The day your sale order is executed is the last day of the holding period, even though delivery and payment may not be made until several days later (settlement date).

If you have purchased shares of the same security on different dates and cannot determine which shares you are selling, the shares purchased at the earliest time are considered the stock sold first. This is the *first-in, first-out* (FIFO) rule.

How Taxes Can Affect Your Net Investment Return

As noted earlier, individual investors and mutual funds typically concentrate on providing maximum pretax returns, which may ignore what matters most: what's left for you after taxes. Where possible, a tax-savvy investor seeks to reduce taxable capital gains and income distributions. Of primary importance to you are your net returns, after taxes. This is your real bottom line.

Your pretax and after-tax returns can be substantially different, and the difference compounds over time. According to The Vanguard Group of Investment Companies, over a recent five-year period, 28 percent of the average yearly return of the ten largest equity funds was lost to taxes. These ten funds provided an average annualized total return for the period of 14.9 percent. After taxes, the average annualized total return decreased to 10.8 percent—a 28 percent difference. The result assumes that all dividend income and capital gains distributions were reinvested after taxes were paid at the highest federal rates in effect during each year and that shares were sold and capital gains taxes were paid at the end of the period.

How to Minimize Your Exposure to Taxes

You can use five simple techniques to minimize the impact of taxes on your investment returns:

1. *Minimize portfolio turnover.* Frequent trading to lock in profits may also have the effect of locking in a continuous stream of tax liabilities. One effective way to minimize portfolio turnover is taking a market index approach to your equity investing. You can do this easily by investing in an index fund, such as an S&P 500 index fund that invests in substantially all of the stocks in the Standard & Poor's 500 Composite Stock Price Index. An index fund buys and holds stocks that track the performance of its designated index. (For more on index funds, see Chapter 35.) This limits stock trading and, therefore, capital gains distributions.

2. *Use a disciplined sell selection method.* Use tax-minimizing techniques such as selling securities in your portfolio with the highest original cost. In addition, when sensible, realize capital losses to help offset any realized capital gains.

3. *Emphasize stocks with low-dividend yields.* If current income is not an important objective for you, invest in a diversified group of stocks that pay little or no dividends. Companies that choose to reinvest their earnings back into the company to finance future growth typically enable you to realize growth of your invested capital, together with deferred taxation.

4. *Invest in tax-exempt securities.* You can avoid federal, state, and municipal income taxes (but not capital gains taxes) entirely by investing in tax-free bonds or bond funds (see Chapter 21).

5. *Invest through a retirement account.* One of the simplest ways to defer taxes and enhance your investment return is to take advantage of retirement plans such as a 401(k), IRA, or other tax-favored arrangement. (For more on tax-funded retirement plans, see Chapter 6.)

Invest the Smart Way

*I*nvestors typically concentrate on achieving maximum pretax returns. But you should develop a tax-efficient investment strategy to minimize your investment portfolio's exposure to taxes. What matters most is what's left for you after taxes.

Building Your Assets with a Tax-Favored Retirement Plan

Government-sponsored individual retirement accounts (IRAs) and 401(k) plans provide two of the best ways to grow your fortune while taking advantage of important tax benefits. The trend in America today is for individuals to take responsibility for funding their own retirement needs. Increasing numbers of businesses are turning away from the pension plans that millions of workers traditionally counted on for retirement income and are asking workers to pay for and manage their own retirement plans.

The assets of 401(k) retirement plans alone probably will surpass the $1 trillion mark in the next two years, according to Access Research, a Windsor, Connecticut, firm that tracks employee benefit programs. The assets of 401(k) plans totaled more than $800 billion at the end of 1996, up from $300 billion in 1990.

Money from all types of retirement plans is responsible for fueling much of the growth of the $3.5 trillion mutual fund industry. Mutual funds have been a good fit for participant-directed retirement plans, because fund companies offer a broad investment choice to the average investor. They also convey information in a way the average investor can understand.

What Are the Tax Benefits?

Contributions made to the plans can be tax-deductible, and earnings grow free of taxation until the proceeds are actually distributed. In planning your own tax-favored retirement plan, many strategies recommended for any long-term investment program apply. Following are some key points to consider:

- *Begin early.* Start putting money aside as soon as possible. The earlier you start, the more time will work for you, and the more you will have for retirement.
- *Contribute generously.* Invest as much as you can afford, up to the limit permitted in the plan that you choose.
- *Invest for growth.* If you can accept moderate risk and retirement is many years away, invest primarily in equities (common stocks), which have provided the best long-term returns.
- *Diversify.* Spread your investment program adequately among securities. Invest in equities for growth, bonds for income, and cash reserves for safety. When you diversify, risk is dramatically reduced.
- *Stay with your program.* Consistency of purpose is a key factor in having a successful retirement plan. Continue your investment program throughout up and down cycles of the stock and bond markets.
- *Remember inflation.* Keep the potential for growth in your plan even after you retire to guard against inflation. A 4 percent inflation rate will reduce the purchasing power of your dollars by half in 20 years.

This chapter highlights the main plans that may be available to you and how you can use them. Many investment brokers and mutual fund companies have plans in which you can participate, often at little or no cost. They will be happy to provide you with free information and everything you need to get started.

Individual Retirement Account (IRA)

The government-sponsored IRA is one of the best tax-advantaged ways to supplement your retirement income. Section 408(a) of the Internal Revenue Code of 1986 describes the individual retirement account, which allows you to establish a long-term retirement program with two important tax advantages:

1. All your earnings accumulate tax-free in your IRA until you begin making withdrawals. Over time, this tax-deferred accumulation will have a major effect on your IRA, causing your assets to grow at a more rapid rate.
2. Because your IRA contributions may be tax-deductible, you may be able to reduce your federal income taxes now.

Under a voluntary IRA program, you may make investment contributions on a regular monthly, quarterly, or annual basis and thereby take advantage of the powerful effect of dollar cost averaging. (For more on dollar cost averaging, see Chapter 3.)

For most people, an IRA is a long-term retirement program, and the investments you select should be made with that thought in mind. According to Ibbotson Associates, the stock market has historically provided investors with an average return of 10 percent per year. In recent years the returns have been higher. For example, in the ten years ending in 1996, the average U.S. equity mutual fund had an average annual total return of 13.30 percent.

Past market performance is no guarantee of future results. But as an illustration, Figure 6.1 shows the potential results of investing $4,000 per year in an IRA investment program for two working spouses over different time frames with an average annual return of 10 percent.

Eligibility. Generally, anyone younger than age 70½ who earns income from employment, including self-employment, may make annual contributions to an IRA.

Amount you may contribute. A maximum of $2,000 or 100 percent of your compensation, whichever is less, may be contributed to your IRA each year.

Your spouse. Because each employed spouse may open a separate IRA and contribute 100 percent of compensation up to $2,000 a year, a working couple can make total contributions of as much as $4,000 annually to their IRAs.

Nonworking spouse. If your spouse earns no compensation for the year, you may be eligible to increase your total IRA contribution by having an additional but separate spousal IRA established for your spouse. With a spousal IRA, your maximum annual IRA contribution

FIGURE 6.1 $4,000 Invested Each Year with a 10 Percent Annual Return

Number of Years Invested	Accumulated Value of the Account
5	$ 26,862
10	70,125
15	139,799
20	252,010
25	432,727
30	723,774
35	1,192,507
40	1,947,407

may be increased to $4,000, which may be split between the separate IRA accounts of you and your nonworking spouse, provided not more than $2,000 is contributed to either account for any one year.

Tax-deductibility.   Your IRA contributions will be deductible for federal income tax purposes if neither you nor your spouse is an active participant in an employer-maintained retirement plan. If one of you is an active participant in such a retirement plan, the deductibility of your IRA contributions will be determined by your adjusted gross income as follows:

- For adjusted gross income in 1998 of less than $50,000 ($35,000 on single returns), your IRA contributions will be fully deductible.
- For adjusted gross incomes above $50,000 ($35,000 on single returns), the deduction for your IRA contributions will be reduced proportionately as your adjusted gross income increases above these limits.
- Income limits for those eligible to make tax-deductible contributions to IRAs will gradually increase from $50,000 to $80,000 for couples and from $30,000 to $50,000 for singles.

You are generally considered an active participant for a tax year if you participate in any employer-maintained retirement plan (including pension, profit sharing, 401(k), simplified employee pension, or Keogh plans) during any part of the year. The Form W-2 you receive from your employer each year should indicate whether you are an active participant in the employer's retirement plan.

If neither you nor your spouse is an active participant in an employer-maintained retirement plan, your IRA contributions will be fully deductible regardless of your income level.

Nondeductible IRA contributions.   You are permitted to make nondeductible contributions to your IRA to the extent you are not eligible to make deductible IRA contributions. Earnings on such nondeductible contributions are not subject to federal income tax until you withdraw them. In the meantime, you will enjoy one of the most important benefits associated with IRAs: compounded, tax-deferred earnings.

IRA-Plus.   If you haven't been able to make deductible IRA contributions because you are covered by a company retirement plan and have income above the limits described earlier, a new IRA option was created by law in 1997. Effective in 1998, you can make nondeductible contributions of up to $2,000 (as can your spouse). Earnings will be tax-free if the money remains in the account for at least five years and is then withdrawn past age 59½ or for educational expenses or for the purchase of your first home.

When IRA contributions may be made.   For each tax year, you can make deductible or nondeductible contributions to your IRA at any time until the due date for filing your income tax return (not including extensions). For most taxpayers, the latest date for any year is April 15 of the following year. But remember, the sooner you contribute to your IRA, the sooner tax-sheltered earnings will accrue.

Contributions are voluntary.   You do not need to make contributions to your IRA every year, nor are you required to make the maximum contribution in any year. You may contribute any amount you wish, provided you don't exceed the limits. However, if you decide in any year not to make the maximum IRA contribution, you may not make up the missed contribution amount in later years.

Age limitation on continuing contributions.   You may make contributions to your IRA for each year you earn compensation until the year you attain age 70½.

Withdrawals from your IRA.   Generally, you may start withdrawals from your IRA as early as age 59½. Withdrawals must begin by April 1 following the year you attain age 70½. Penalty-free withdrawals may also be made before age 59½ for educational expenses and a first-time home purchase.

Taxation of withdrawals.   Withdrawals from your IRA will be taxed as ordinary income, with the exception that if you make any non-deductible contributions to your IRA, your IRA withdrawals will be treated partly as a nontaxable return of your nondeductible IRA contributions and partly as a taxable distribution of your IRA earnings and any deductible IRA contributions.

Withdrawals before age 59½.   Because an IRA is intended to provide for your retirement, the law imposes an additional tax of 10 percent if you withdraw prior to age 59½ for reasons other than your disability, educational expenses, or a first-time home purchase. This 10 percent tax is applied to the taxable amount of your withdrawal and is in addition to the ordinary income tax you pay on your withdrawal. The 10 percent additional tax will not apply to distributions made to your beneficiary in the event of your death. Also, the 10 percent tax will not apply to certain installment or annuity payments made for your life or life expectancy or for the joint lives or life expectancies of you and your beneficiary, regardless of when these payments begin.

Methods of distribution.   Withdrawals from your IRA may be made in one or more lump-sum payments or in regular monthly, quarterly, or annual installments. Installment payments may be paid over a period that does not exceed your life expectancy or the joint life expectancies of you and your beneficiary.

In event of your death.   Any amount in your IRA at the time of your death will be distributed to your designated beneficiary(ies). If you do not designate a beneficiary or if your designated beneficiary(ies) dies before you do, your estate will become the beneficiary.

Transfers and rollovers.   A transfer occurs when IRA assets are transferred directly from one custodian to another. You are permitted to transfer your existing IRA assets from one custodian to another without paying taxes. Such a direct transfer may be made as often as you wish. A rollover occurs when you receive IRA assets from one custodian then move the assets to another custodian, for example, from a bank to a brokerage firm. If you receive a distribution of assets from an existing

IRA, you may make a tax-free rollover contribution of all or part of the assets you receive to another IRA. The rollover must be completed within 60 days after you receive the distribution from your existing IRA to avoid paying income or penalty taxes. You may make only one such tax-free rollover every 12 months.

401(k) Plans

You may be eligible for a 401(k) plan, now available to employees of large and medium-sized companies, and an increasing number of small companies. In many major corporations, pension plans are rapidly being overtaken by these plans, which require employees to put in their own money for retirement and make their own decisions on how the funds will be invested. Thus, an employee may elect to reduce his or her taxable compensation with contributions to a 401(k) plan where those amounts will accumulate tax-free. Employers often match these amounts with employer contributions. According to Sanford C. Bernstein & Company, more than 40 million Americans now have 401(k) plans, up from hardly any just 15 years ago. Employees of nonprofit organizations may be eligible for a similar or 403(b) plan.

Named after a section of the Internal Revenue Code that authorizes it, 401(k) plans have been available since 1978. Under such plans, employees put a percentage of their pretax earnings into an investment account, where the money grows free of taxation until retirement. Most 401(k) plans offer a selection of investment options, usually mutual funds. Expanding from the three or four funds that used to be standard, employees now often can choose from among one dozen, two dozen, or more mutual funds. Some employers have also begun to embrace a radically different option, even if it can be risky for many workers. It is a self-managed 401(k) account that lets an employee choose from thousands of stocks, bonds, and mutual funds, while still being able to invest in the plan's other choices.

At an employee's retirement, the 401(k) plan provides one lump-sum distribution, the size of which depends on how much the employee saved during the years and how effectively it was invested. Like other retirement plans, assets may be rolled over or transferred to an IRA.

Yet many participants are not setting aside enough money in their 401(k) plans and they are poorly investing what they do save. In addition, participating employees frequently turn to these retirement accounts for cash to cover everything from houses to cars to medical bills. Remember, a successful retirement plan requires a long-term commitment to savings.

Invest the Smart Way

*I*RAs and 401(k) plans offered by employers represent two excellent vehicles for building your retirement funds on a highly tax-favored basis. While not all wage earners qualify for tax-deductible IRA contributions, nearly all can take advantage of the tax-deferred accumulation privilege. So begin early and contribute generously.

CHAPTER 7

The Importance of Market Indexes—and How They Work

Market indexes show the general direction of fluctuations in the securities markets and reflect the historical continuity of security price movements. While this information will not necessarily tell you whether the stocks in your portfolio are up or down, it is useful to understand how the indexes work, for they are commonly used as benchmarks for judging the performance of individual stocks, bonds, and mutual funds. So-called market *averages* are not really averages anymore. The term *index* is more appropriate, because the numbers given, usually called *points,* should not be mistaken for dollar-per-share prices of stocks. Points refer to units of movement in the average, which is a composite of weighted dollar values.

Indexes track stocks in particular industry sectors, in specific markets, or of a certain capitalization. For instance, one index tracks gold stocks. Another tracks stocks of companies engaged in the distribution and transmission of natural gas. An index exists for each of several exchanges where stocks are traded, including indexes for stocks that trade on the New York Stock Exchange (NYSE), the American Stock Exchange (AMEX), and the over-the-counter market (OTC). One index tracks small capitalization stocks, one tracks large capitalization stocks, and another tracks all stocks traded in the United States. This chapter describes the more widely known indexes.

Price-Weighted and Market Value–Weighted Averages

An average or index is referred to as being *price-weighted* when it is weighted by the market price of each security included in the average. Thus, securities with high market prices tend to be more heavily weighted and have more influence on changes in a price-weighted average. The Dow Jones averages are examples of price-weighted averages.

An index is said to be *market value–weighted* when it is adjusted according to the market value of each security included in the average. The greater a firm's number of shares outstanding and the higher the price of the shares, the greater the weight of that security in a market value–weighted average. The S&P 500 index is market value–weighted.

Dow Jones Industrial Average

The best-known and most widely quoted index is the Dow Jones Industrial Average (DJIA), published by Dow Jones & Company, often referred to simply as "the Dow." You can hardly avoid hearing about the Dow's progress as newscasters comment daily on radio and television news programs.

For a century, industrial stocks have proliferated, and the Dow has come a long way. It easily has become the best-known and most often quoted of all the averages. It is also the most widely used stock market indicator, although the S&P 500 has become an important standard for many.

The DJIA is a price-weighted average of 30 actively traded blue chip stocks consisting primarily of industrial companies. The components represent between 15 percent and 20 percent of the market value of NYSE stocks.

The DJIA is calculated by adding the closing prices of the component stocks and using a divisor that is adjusted for stock splits and stock dividends, as well as for substitutions and mergers. The average is quoted in points, not dollars. In March 1997, the Dow Jones Industrials consisted of the following companies:

AlliedSignal
Aluminum Company of America
American Express Company
AT&T Corporation
Boeing Company
Caterpillar, Inc.
Chevron Corporation
Coca-Cola Company
Disney (Walt) Company
dupont (E.I.) de Nemours & Co.
Eastman Kodak Company
Exxon Corporation
General Electric Company
General Motors
Goodyear Tire & Rubber
    Company
Hewlett-Packard Company

International Business Machines
    Corporation
International Paper Company
Johnson & Johnson
McDonald's Corporation
Merck & Company, Inc.
Minnesota Mining &
    Manufacturing Company
Morgan (J.P.) & Company, Inc.
Philip Morris Companies, Inc.
Proctor & Gamble Company
Sears Roebuck and Company
Travelers Group, Inc.
Union Carbide Corporation
United Technologies Corporation
Wal-Mart Stores, Inc.

The DJIA is simply a statistical compilation that reflects combined, not individual, performances. The two great advantages of the DJIA are simplicity and continuity. The present high level of the average is a result of its continuity. Its base never has changed, because to do so would, in effect, start a new average.

A problem of the DJIA is that it exaggerates market movements because it is described in points and runs more than 100 times the straight average price of industrial stocks. Over the years, stocks have been split, but the DJIA has not. It has been suggested that Dow Jones & Company split the industrials one-for-ten or move the decimal one place to the left. The general opinion, however, is that the average has gone to its lofty height and moves up or down strictly according to arithmetic. If the arithmetic were changed, continuity would be lost—and continuity is the average's greatest advantage.

Remember that the market "averages" really are not averages any-more. They were originally and still are referred to as such. Although they are useful measures of the overall movement of the stock market, the numbers themselves should not be mistaken for dollar-per-share prices of stocks. This applies not only to the DJIA but to all stock indexes.

The reason for the disparity is *stock splits,* which occur when a company believes that the per-share price of its stock is too high for broad investor appeal. The company then arbitrarily splits the high-priced shares, creating more lower-priced shares. For example, if a stock sell-ing for $100 is split two-for-one, the new price will be $50, other fac-tors remaining unchanged. Of course, each owner of each share of the old $100 stock must be given an additional share of stock so the value of his or her holding will not be reduced.

Stock splitting, which occurs year after year, would distort the aver-ages unless statistical market value–weighted adjustments were not also made to compensate for them. Thus, the Dow Jones averages are not dollar averages of current market prices but movement indicators, kept essentially undistorted for more than 100 years.

The DJIA, originally consisting of 12 stocks in 1896, was increased to 20 in 1916 and then to its present level of 30 in 1928. Whenever any particular component stock for any reason becomes unrepresentative of the American industrial sector, a substitution is made and the average adjusted, just as when a split occurs.

Critics sometimes charge that the DJIA includes only 30 companies and so fails to reflect the movement of hundreds of other stock prices. But these 30 securities are chosen as representative of the broad market and of American industry. The companies are major factors in their industries, and their stocks are widely held by both individuals and institutions. Changes in the components are made rarely, often as a result of mergers, but occasionally they may be made to effect a better representation. The most recent changes occurred in 1997, when four stocks were removed from the average and substituted with four other stocks.

Other Widely Used Market Indexes

Over time, especially in recent years, the number of market indexes has proliferated. In addition to its industrial average, Dow Jones & Company itself now publishes a transportation average, a utility aver-age, and a composite average of all three. Other market indexes have been developed by investment services firms, an industry association, and even mutual fund companies. Some of the more widely known indexes follow:

American Gas Association (AGA) Stock Index.   The AGA Stock Index contains approximately 107 publicly traded stocks of com-panies engaged in the natural gas distribution and transmission industry.

Benham North American Gold Equities Index. This index consists of 28 stocks of North American companies engaged in exploring for, mining, processing, fabricating, or otherwise dealing in gold.

Dow Jones Transportation Average (DJTA). This index is a price-weighted average of the stocks of 20 large companies in the transportation business, including airlines, railroads, and trucking. From 1897 to 1969, this indicator was called the Dow Jones Railroad Average.

Dow Jones Utility Average (DJUA). This is a price-weighted average composed of 15 geographically representative and well-established gas and electric utility companies.

Dow Jones 65 Composite Stock Average. This average consists of the 30 stocks in the DJIA, the 20 stocks in the DJTA, and the 15 stocks in the DJUA. This average is significant because it is a combination of the three blue chip averages and, therefore, gives a good indication of the overall direction of the largest, most established companies.

Lehman Brothers Aggregate Bond Index. This index measures total investment return (capital changes plus income) provided by a universe of fixed-income securities, weighted by the total market value of each security. More than 6,000 issues (including bonds, notes, debentures, and mortgage issues) are included in the index.

Morgan Stanley Capital International Europe (Free) Index. This index is a diversified, market value–weighted index comprising approximately 575 companies located in 13 European countries. The "free" index includes only shares that U.S. investors are "free to purchase."

Morgan Stanley Capital International Pacific Index. This is a diversified, market value–weighted Pacific Basin index consisting of approximately 525 companies located in Australia, Japan, Hong Kong, New Zealand, and Singapore. The Japanese stock market represents about 85 percent of the market value.

Morgan Stanley Capital International Europe, Australia, and Far East (Free) Index.

This is a broadly diversified international index consisting of more than 1,000 equity securities of companies located outside the United States.

Nasdaq National Market System Composite Index.

This is a market value–weighted index composed of all the stocks traded on the National Market System (NMS) of the OTC market, which is supervised by the National Association of Securities Dealers (NASD).

New York Stock Exchange Composite Index.

This index is market value–weighted and includes all NYSE stocks.

Russell 2000 Small Stock Index.

This is a broadly diversified, small capitalization index consisting of approximately 2,000 common stocks. The average capitalization (number of outstanding shares times the market price per share) of stocks in this index is less than $500 million.

The Schwab 1000 Index.

This index is composed of the common stocks of the 1,000 largest U.S. corporations (excluding investment companies) as measured by market capitalization.

Standard & Poor's 500 Composite Stock Price Index.

The S&P 500 measures the *total investment return* (change in market price plus income) of 500 common stocks, which are chosen by Standard & Poor's Corporation on a statistical basis. The 500 securities, most of which trade on the NYSE, represent about 70 percent of the market value of all U.S. common stocks. Typically, companies included in the S&P 500 are the largest and most dominant firms in their industries.

Value Line Composite Index.

This equally weighted geometric average is composed of the approximately 1,700 stocks tracked by the *Value Line Investment Survey* and traded on the NYSE, AMEX, and OTC market.

Wilshire 5000 Index.

This index consists of all regularly and publicly traded U.S. stocks; it provides a complete proxy for the U.S. stock market. More than 6,000 stocks are included in the index. It is used to measure how all stocks are doing as a group, as opposed to a particular segment of the market.

Wilshire Small Cap Index.   This index consists of common stock of 250 companies with an average market capitalization of $400 million, chosen on the basis of market capitalization, liquidity, and industry group representation.

Invest the Smart Way

Securities market indexes give a general idea of fluctuations in the securities markets and reflect the historical continuity of security price movements. Understanding how the indexes work can help you invest successfully because they are commonly used as benchmarks for judging the performance of individual stocks, bonds, and mutual funds.

CHAPTER 8

Avoiding Probate without a Trust and without a Will

*R*ecent legislation enacted by some states makes it possible to transfer your stock, bond, and mutual fund assets directly to your beneficiaries outside of probate and without the necessity of a trust or will. You can designate beneficiaries for any one or more of your individual or joint nonretirement accounts that are held by a mutual fund company or securities broker that offers a *directed beneficiary arrangement* (DBA), regardless of your state of residence. Following your death (or the death of the last surviving joint owner, if your accounts are jointly registered), ownership of these accounts will be transferred directly to the beneficiaries you specify—avoiding probate and without the formalities and expense of a trust.

Under a DBA, you retain complete lifetime control over your accounts. Your designated beneficiaries have no rights to your accounts until after your death or the death of the last surviving owner. You can change your beneficiaries or revoke the arrangement at any time, simply by writing to the mutual fund or broker.

There is no change in how accounts covered by a DBA are taxed. They are taxed the same way as "regular" accounts. You will be subject to current income tax on any earnings, and these accounts ordinarily will be subject to estate tax upon your death. You should incur no gift taxes as a result of the arrangement, because you can change your beneficiary at any time.

Is probate really a big burden? Probate is the court-supervised process of collecting and distributing a person's property after death. There are three unhappy consequences of having your investment assets probated under the jurisdiction of the court:

1. *Probate is time-consuming.* In a survey of knowledgeable attorneys across the country, the time required to probate a will was indicated to be from two to five years!

2. *Probate attracts publicity.* Private matters become newspaper headlines. Local reporters cover the probate court. Also, from probate court records, lists of widows are compiled and sold to people who prey on beneficiaries to separate them from their money.

3. *Probate is costly.* The cost of estate administration can be exceedingly high. In the case of small estates ($10,000 to $20,000), it can average 20 percent. On medium-sized estates in the $100,000 range, it runs about 10 percent. For larger estates, the percentages will be smaller, but the amounts can be very large.

It can be very much to your advantage to avoid the time, cost, and publicity involved in the probate process. Simplicity is the key advantage of a DBA, but it is not a substitute for a comprehensive estate plan. A DBA allows you to transfer assets directly to your chosen beneficiaries, just by completing a short form. However, unlike a will or trust, the DBA does not permit you to impose special terms and conditions on the way your beneficiaries receive and use these assets, nor does it enable you to take advantage of sophisticated tax-planning techniques that could substantially reduce the impact of estate taxes on your assets.

How a Directed Beneficiary Arrangement Works

A DBA permits you to register beneficiaries for your individual or joint mutual fund or brokerage accounts. Following your death, or the death of the account's last surviving joint owner, ownership of your DBA accounts passes directly to your named beneficiaries. These assets bypass the probate process.

Under the Vanguard Directed Beneficiary Plan, offered by the Vanguard Group (800-662-2739), individual accounts and joint tenants with rights of survivorship accounts invested in Vanguard mutual funds or through Vanguard's brokerage services are eligible to be covered by the plan. The plan cannot be used for IRAs and other retirement accounts or for community property accounts and joint accounts held as tenants in common.

To cover a joint account, all joint owners must sign the directed beneficiary plan application. Ownership of a joint account passes to the plan beneficiaries after the death of the last surviving owner. All living joint owners must consent in writing to any plan changes, including beneficiary revisions or termination of the plan.

The Vanguard plan permits you to make telephone exchanges involving identically registered mutual fund accounts covered by the plan, if permitted by the applicable Vanguard funds. If you establish a new investment account by telephone exchange from a plan account, the new account will also be covered by the plan. But exchanges by telephone are not permitted between plan accounts and any accounts not covered by the plan.

Following your death, it is the plan beneficiary's responsibility to provide a certified copy of your death certificate (or death certificates for all joint account owners), a signed Form W-9, and a completed copy of a Transfer of Shares to New Owner form. In some states, it may be necessary to also provide a state inheritance tax waiver or proof of payment of estate taxes. Under normal circumstances, the accounts are transferred to your beneficiary immediately upon presentation of these documents.

Other Considerations

Would it be easier to simply name as joint owner the person you want as beneficiary? If you name a joint owner to an investment account, then that person is on equal footing with you with respect to the account. Once named, you cannot unilaterally remove your joint owner from the account, and the survivor of the two of you will assume ownership of the entire account. In addition, under certain conditions, you may incur gift taxes by naming a joint owner to your account. By contrast, if you adopt a DBA, your designated beneficiary has no rights until after your death, and there are no gift tax implications. During your lifetime, you can change your plan beneficiary at any time by written notice. You can also revoke the plan at any time.

In the event there is a conflict between the DBA and a will or trust you may also have, the DBA will supersede your will or trust. This means your plan beneficiaries will receive your plan accounts, even if your will or trust provides differently. To avoid any confusion or disputes among your heirs and to expedite the transfer of your account, you should amend any inconsistent estate documents before establishing a DBA.

Invest the Smart Way

A directed beneficiary arrangement provides a way for you to pass ownership of your DBA accounts, without probate, to your designated plan beneficiaries following your death (or the death of the last surviving joint owner of your DBA accounts). The DBA will supersede any conflicting provision you may have made in a will or trust. However, your DBA will not supersede any rights that creditors or other persons may have to your plan accounts under applicable law.

PART TWO

Investing the Smart Way in Stocks

CHAPTER 9

Stock Market Strategies You Can Use

*A*ll stock market strategies have but one purpose—to guide you in your quest to realize superior returns on your invested capital. The extraordinary volatility of the securities markets reminds us of how important portfolio planning is to sound long-term investing.

Over the long term (from 1926 to 1996), returns provided by common stocks have averaged +10.5 percent annually. But this average return masks a great deal of volatility, as returns from common stocks have fluctuated within a very wide band. In the 71 years from 1926 through 1996, the stock market has provided annual returns ranging from a low of −43.3 percent (in 1931) to a high of +53.9 percent (in 1933).

This extreme volatility is the chief risk of investing in common stocks, but it is a risk that tends to recede from investors' memories after a lengthy period of generally rising stock prices, such as the period that began in August 1982 and continued through early 1997. Those investors new to investing in common stocks may underestimate the volatility of common stocks because volatility has been muted in recent years.

Time greatly reduces, but does not eliminate, the volatility in returns from stocks. According to Ibbotson Associates, over five-year periods (1926–1930, 1927–1931, and so on) from 1926 through 1996, average annual returns on stocks ranged from −12.5 percent to +23.9 percent. Over ten-year periods, the range of average annual returns has been narrower, from −0.9 percent to +20.1 percent.

Market Approaches

Most strategies used to invest in the stock market fall into three general categories:

1. Fundamental analysis
2. Technical analysis
3. Buy and hold the market

Fundamental Analysis

This investment approach is primarily concerned with value. Fundamental analysis examines factors that determine a company's expected future earnings and dividends and the dependability of those earnings and dividends. It then attempts to put a value on the stock in accordance with its findings. A fundamentalist then seeks out stocks that are a good value, meaning stocks that are priced low relative to their perceived value. The assumption is that the stock market will later recognize the value of the stock and its price will increase accordingly.

Technical Analysis

The technical analyst attempts to predict the future price of a stock or the future direction of the stock market based on past price and trading volume changes. This approach assumes that stock prices and the stock market follow discernible patterns, and if the beginning of a pattern can be identified, the balance of the pattern can be predicted well enough to yield returns in excess of the general market. Most academic studies of this approach have concluded that investing based on purely technical analysis does not work.

Buy and Hold the Market

The buy-and-hold-the-market approach is the benchmark against which any other approach to the market should be measured. This strategy provides the returns that would be obtained by buying and holding the stock market, often defined as the S&P 500. Of course, no individual investor would buy all 500 stocks that make up the index (although this can be achieved by buying shares in an S&P 500 index mutual fund, as discussed in Chapter 35). By investing in a large number of well-diversified stocks, however, investors can build portfolios that closely resemble the S&P 500.

The buy-and-hold-the-market investment approach is used as a benchmark because no other investment approach based on analysis is valid unless it can outperform the market over the long run. When an investment produces a return that is above the market return with the same risk, the difference between the two returns is referred to as an *excess return.* The excess return represents the added value of the approach.

Buying on Margin

If you feel so optimistic about a stock that you are willing to take on additional risk in the hope of enhancing your return, you can utilize a technique called buying *on margin,* or with borrowed funds. According to rules set by the Federal Reserve, brokers can lend you up to half the money you need to buy stocks, as long as they have collateral of yours to seize in case your stocks lose value. The collateral must be in the form of securities or cash. The broker will charge you interest on the loan, typically about a percentage point over the prime rate.

By doubling the amount of your purchase (by borrowing), you can make twice as much money if your stock goes up than you can make by paying for your stock in full. But this coin has two sides; if the stock you bought on margin declines in value, you will lose twice as much money as would be the case if you had paid cash in full. For you to break even, your stock must increase in value by the amount of your interest costs. If your stock value drops in half, you will be hit by a *margin call.* When you receive a margin call from your broker, you must put up additional collateral to cover your loan or your position in the stock will be sold immediately. If this happens, you will have lost your entire investment. Clearly, buying on margin is a risky technique.

Selling Short

Even riskier than buying on margin is a technique called *selling short.* You might want to risk going short if you think the price of a stock will drop. If you are right and your stock does drop in price, you can make a lot of money. But if you are wrong and the stock goes up, your losses are unlimited because the stock you have shorted can rise indefinitely.

Here's the way selling short works: Perhaps you believe the sales of a particular company are slowing dramatically and the company will show a loss at the next reporting period, causing the price of the stock to drop sharply. To sell the stock short, you essentially borrow the shares from someone who owns them, usually your broker, with the promise that you will return the shares later. You then sell the borrowed shares at the current market price, which you think is too high.

When the price drops (Congratulations—you were right!), you buy the same number of shares of the stock back and return them to the lender. This is known as *covering* your short position. Your profit is the difference between the price you originally sold the stock for and the price at which you bought it back.

But suppose the company's earnings report turns out to be better than expected and the share price soars—you will be very unhappy. You must cover your short position, buying the shares back at a higher price than at which you sold and taking a loss. The higher the price goes, the greater will be your loss. Short selling, like buying on margin, should be done only if you have nerves of steel. You can get poor in a hurry if you're wrong.

How Efficient Is the Stock Market?

According to the efficient market theory, stock prices in an efficient market reflect all publicly available information concerning that stock and so are extremely close to the true value of the stock. This does not mean that stock prices reflect the stock's true value at all times, but that stock prices on average reflect the true value. Variations about this average price may exist.

The random walk theory says that these variations are unpredictable; sometimes they are positive and sometimes they are negative. Because they are unpredictable, they cannot be used to obtain excess returns. This theory concerning random variation in prices purports to explain the short-term price fluctuations that occur seemingly without cause.

But we reviewed the two widely discussed and controversial stock market theories, the random walk and efficient market theories, in Chapter 1. Interesting as those theories are, the question remains: Is the stock market an efficient market? If it is, there would be no point in pursuing the fundamental approach that seeks to find stocks that are selling significantly above or below their value. The argument would be that stock prices vary randomly around their "true" value. Investors who believe the stock market is efficient would concentrate on developing the more efficient portfolio, rather than concentrating on specific stock selection. An efficient portfolio is one that provides returns closest to the market's return at a given level of market risk. The investor simply determines the amount of risk that he or she is willing to bear and then builds a portfolio accordingly.

Investors who believe the market is inefficient proceed on the assumption that variations in the way people receive and evaluate information cause the prices of some stocks to deviate significantly from their true value. Therefore, they see an opportunity for finding underpriced and overpriced stocks through diligent analysis, and being able to outperform a buy-and-hold-the-market strategy.

Based on substantial research evidence, many analysts believe that the market often is inefficient, and that there are opportunities for outperforming the market. The excess return potential appears to be in the range of 2 percent to 6 percent annually. Over a lifetime of investing, even a relatively small additional return can lead to substantially additional wealth.

The Effect of Transaction Costs

Don't ignore the impact of transaction costs when comparing the different approaches to investing. Take into account three important factors when trading stocks:

1. Commissions
2. The bid-ask spread
3. Taxes

Let's look at a typical transaction. You own 100 shares of stock in company A and decide to sell them and buy 100 shares of stock in company B. Assume that the last trade on the exchange for each stock was for $25 a share. When you consider these three factors, the cost of making the switch looks something like the following:

- *Commissions.* The total commission cost for selling 100 shares of A and buying 100 shares of B would range from $50 (using a discount broker) to $125 (using a full-service broker). This represents a commission of from 2 percent to 5 percent of your $2,500 investment. (Note that deep-discount brokers charge as little as $25 or less for a stock purchase or sale).

- *Bid-ask spread.* The cost of your switch is increased by the bid-ask spread, which is the difference between the price (bid) at which a stock can be bought and the price (ask) at which it can be sold. For example, for both company A and company B, the current spread may be 24⅞ (ask) to 25⅛ (bid). In this case, you would receive $24.875 a share for selling and pay $25.125 for buying B. You have just suffered another 1 percent charge. The difference between bid and ask prices is the fee retained by the market maker or specialist. An actively traded stock will have a narrower spread than a stock that is thinly traded.
- *Taxes.* If you enjoyed a profit on your sale of company A's stock, you will have to pay a tax. Of course, taxes would have to be paid eventually, but if they are deferred (by holding on to the shares), you will continue to earn a return on the eventual liability. Comparing a one-year holding period with a ten-year holding period, the value of deferring taxes could be worth another 0.5 percent each year.

So switching can be expensive. You pay somewhere between 3 percent and 6 percent to switch from one stock to another. This does not mean it should not be done, just that the new stock must perform sufficiently better to overcome the setback. Investors who use investment techniques that result in turning over their entire portfolio several times a year must outperform the market substantially just to match a buy-and-hold approach.

Setting Your Objecti1ves

It is clear that to be successful, you must set an objective in terms of what is to be achieved and the anticipated time frame in which to accomplish the objective.

Short-Term versus Long-Term Risk

As discussed earlier, how long you hold an investment has an important effect on the degree of risk you undertake. In this context, consider risk as the likelihood that your capital will diminish from the time of your initial purchase to the end of the holding period.

As noted in the beginning of this chapter, while the stock market can be risky in the short run, time has a moderating effect. The longer you hold a portfolio of stocks, the lower your chances of losing money and the greater the odds of earning a return close to the long-term average.

Real Stock Market Risk

People do, of course, lose money in the market. The following are some of the real risks of investing in the stock market:

1. Short-term investing is risky. An investor has about a 30 percent chance of showing a loss at the end of one year. This would happen more often if taxes and transaction costs are figured in.
2. Many investors are not sufficiently diversified, taking on more risk and incurring more losses than the market as a whole.
3. Many investors speculate ("play the market") in an attempt to make large short-term profits by trading their stocks frequently and by trying to predict short-term market swings (timing the market). Because of high transaction costs, most speculators lose money, even in a market with an overall upward trend.

Invest the Smart Way

*I*nvesting in a diversified portfolio of common stocks offers an outstanding opportunity to accumulate wealth through growth at relatively low risk. The stock market is risky for short-term holding periods and for speculators, but as an investor's holding period goes beyond five years, risk is greatly diminished. There have been no losing 15-, 20-, or 25-year periods since 1926.

CHAPTER 10

Discovering Great Stock Market Opportunities

*T*he proliferation of state lotteries across the country and the media attention focused on the huge jackpots are ample evidence of our desire to get rich quickly. But the chances of an individual to cash in big are remote.

In the Florida lottery, for example, one lucky player won more than $30 million in 1997. But the odds of winning the grand prize are just 1 in 13,983,816!

Fortunately, your chances of getting rich in the stock market are better—a lot better. The main requirements are common sense and patience. Part of using common sense is understanding that the stock market is not a get-rich-quick scheme. You can get rich if you have a clear objective, concentrate on the long term, develop a diversified portfolio of securities, and stick with your plan.

This chapter is designed to give you a guided tour through some of the investment opportunities offered by the New York Stock Exchange (NYSE), the American Stock Exchange (AMEX), and the National Association of Securities Dealers Automated Quotations (Nasdaq).

Getting Started

Always base your investment decisions on your own particular financial position, risk comfort level, and goals. Remember, no one is as interested in you and your financial situation as you are. So listen, learn, and consult with people you trust. But in the end, make your own decisions. If you do not understand a finance or investment term, consult the extensive glossary at the end of this book.

You will want to answer several questions before making your first investment in the stock market:

Is capital appreciation your objective?

If so, you will seek out investments with the potential to grow in value to produce capital gains. Along with the appreciation of the asset's value, you will want to take into consideration reinvestment of dividends and interest.

Is income your objective?

If so, you will want to identify investments whose primary feature is to provide regular income. You will want to know if it produces an income of fixed payments, or if you can expect an income stream of gradually increasing payments.

What about inflation?

If the value of an investment can be expected to rise at the same rate or at a rate higher than the rate of inflation, the investment is said to be inflation-sensitive.

Are there tax considerations?

Are you looking for an investment to be included in a tax-deferred retirement account? Such accounts include IRAs, 401(k) plans, and other qualified pension or profit-sharing plans.

Can you borrow against it?

This question involves the general value of an investment as collateral for a loan. Borrowing can be a way of raising cash when an investment cannot readily be sold or when it may not be the right time to sell. An investment also can be used in a margin account with a broker. This gives you leverage, the ability to control a greater value of securities than the amount of cash you have available.

Stock Market Investments

You can choose from a number of investment alternatives traded in the securities markets and available through a broker. (For tips on minimizing brokerage costs, see Chapter 4.) Following are the major categories, with a brief description of each.

Closed-End Funds

A closed-end fund is an investment company with a relatively fixed amount of capital, whose shares are traded on a securities exchange or in the over-the-counter (OTC) market. Unlike a mutual fund, a closed-end fund issues a limited number of shares and does not redeem those that are outstanding. The value of a closed-end fund's shares rises and falls in the marketplace based on the value of the fund's portfolio as well as investor confidence and other market factors. Shares of closed-end funds usually sell at a premium to or discount from the value of their underlying portfolios.

If you are seeking an investment that will grow in value, select a fund having appreciation as its primary objective. Bond funds generally have an objective of providing income. *Dual-purpose funds* have two classes of stock, with common shareholders benefiting from all the capital gains and preferred shareholders receiving all the interest and dividend income. (For more about closed-end funds, see Chapter 37.)

Common Stocks

For total return (capital gains and dividend income), no publicly traded investment offers more potential over the long term than common stock.

Common stock represents the basic equity ownership in a corporation. A shareholder normally is entitled to vote for directors and in other important matters and to share in the wealth created by the corporation's business activities. Shareholders participate in the appreciation of share values and in dividends declared out of earnings that remain after debt obligations and preferred stock dividends are met.

The market values of shares in publicly held corporations are based primarily on investor expectations of future earnings and dividends. These expectations and the resulting stock values often are influenced by forecasts of business activity in general and by so-called investor psychology, which reflects the current business and economic environment. The relationship of market price to a company's actual or expected earnings is called the *price-earnings (PE) ratio,* or *multiple.* For example, a stock selling at $60 a share with earnings of $5 a share is said to be selling at a PE ratio of 12 times earnings, or a multiple of 12.

Stocks of young, rapidly growing companies tend to be volatile, have high PE ratios, and usually carry a high degree of risk. Such companies seldom pay dividends. Instead, dividends are reinvested to finance growth. As opposed to these growth stocks, stocks of older, established companies with histories of regular earnings and dividend payments tend to have more price stability and low PE multiples. Some of these stocks would be characterized as *blue chips;* those paying out substantial dividends are called *income stocks.*

Convertible Securities

Some bonds and preferred stocks are convertible into common stock, usually of the issuer. These convertible securities offer both fixed income and capital appreciation potential. They pay a fixed dividend or rate of interest and are convertible into common stock at a specified price or conversion ratio. The yield on convertibles normally is less than that of nonconvertible bonds or preferreds, and the potential for capital gains is less than with a common stock investment.

Convertibles usually offer less credit risk and market risk than common stock while providing an opportunity for an investor to participate in the future success of the corporation into whose common shares they can be exchanged. Convertible bonds and convertible preferred stock have the same priority of claim on the earnings and assets of a corporation as regular bonds and preferreds. In terms of priority in claims against the corporation's earnings and assets, bonds take precedence over preferred stock, and both take precedence over common stock.

Consider buying a convertible security if your investment objective is capital appreciation and if you want the greater yield and safety of bonds and preferred stocks. Remember, though, because growth is a key feature, yield is less than on a straight bond or preferred stock. Convertibles tend to rise in value with increasing common stock prices, so they also represent a hedge against inflation. (For a full discussion of convertibles, see Chapter 23.)

Foreign Stocks

You can take advantage of opportunities occurring where economies or industry sectors may be growing faster than those in the United States by investing in foreign stocks. These are securities of foreign issuers denominated in foreign currencies. Total returns can be increased through profits on currency movements, but remember, this also means additional risk.

American depositary receipts (ADRs) provide a convenient way to invest in foreign stocks. These negotiable receipts are issued by U.S.

banks and represent actual shares held in their foreign branches. ADRs are traded actively on the major stock exchanges and in the OTC market. There still are currency risks and foreign withholding taxes, but the depositary pays dividends and capital gains in U.S. dollars and handles splits, stock dividends, and rights offerings. Trading inconveniences and custodial problems that exist with trading in foreign stocks are eliminated with ADRs. (For more information on ADRs, see Chapter 17.)

You also can buy foreign stocks through your broker in foreign markets. Depending on the issue and the market, problems include inadequate financial information and regulation, high minimum purchase requirements, higher transaction costs, taxes, possible illiquidity, political risk, and possible currency losses. Unless you are able to take big risks and are sophisticated in the ways of international interest rates and foreign exchange, this avenue of investment may not be a wise one for you to take. International diversification can be readily achieved on a much lower level of risk by investing in closed-end or open-end mutual funds.

Most foreign stock shares traded through ADRs represent solid, established companies, and volatility has tended to be low. Thus these foreign equities on average may normally be safer than many domestic issues. Adverse currency fluctuations, however, introduce an added element of risk.

If your investment objective is growth of capital, foreign stocks offer you the potential for both capital and currency appreciation. From an income perspective, foreign stocks generally have lower dividend yields than U.S. stocks, and exchange-rate fluctuations are a factor in expected returns.

Put and Call Option Contracts

An *option contract* gives the owner the right, for a price, called a *premium,* to buy or sell an underlying stock or financial instrument at a specified price, called the *exercise* or *strike* price, before a specified expiration date.

A *put* is an option to sell, and a *call* is an option to buy. Options sellers are called *writers.* If they own the underlying security, they are called *covered* writers; they are called *naked* writers if they do not.

Options are traded on national stock and commodity exchanges and also in the OTC market. Those listed on the exchanges have greater visibility and are less expensive than those traded over the counter, which are individually negotiated and less liquid. Listed options are available on stocks, stock indexes, debt instruments, foreign currencies, and different types of futures.

Options make it possible for an investor to control a large amount of value with a much smaller amount of money at risk. Options provide leverage, so a small percentage change in the value of a financial instrument can result in a much larger percentage change in the value of an option. Thus, large gains and losses are possible. Options usually are bought and sold, then allowed to expire without ever being exercised. They are financial instruments with lives of their own.

Option prices are determined mainly by the following:

- The relationship between the exercise price and the market price of the underlying security
- The time remaining before the option expires
- The volatility of the underlying security

Consider using options only if you are interested in speculating. Because a small change in a stock price causes a higher percentage change in a related option price, options can give you a substantial amount of leverage. Profits can be great, but losses can mount quickly if the underlying stock does not move in the right direction. Income in the form of premiums you receive from the sale of covered options can add to your income return on the underlying investment. Remember that if you write (sell) an option on a security you own, you may be forced to sell the underlying security if the price moves in the wrong direction.

Preferred Stocks

Preferred stock is an equity that includes features of both common stocks and bonds. Because it is not debt, however, it is riskier than bonds.

The dividends on preferred stock are usually a fixed percentage of par value or a fixed dollar amount. Thus, shares are sensitive to interest rate fluctuations. Like bonds, prices go up when interest rates go down, and vice versa. Preferred dividends, however, are not a contractual expense of the issuer. Although they are payable before common stock dividends, they can be skipped if earnings are low. Again, if the issuer goes bankrupt, although the claims of preferred shareholders come before common shareholders, they do not share in assets until bondholders are paid in full.

Preferred issues are designed for insurance companies and other institutional investors that, as corporations, benefit from an 80 percent tax exclusion on dividends earned. For individuals, though, their fully taxable yields are not much better than that of comparable bonds, and they lack the greater degree of safety afforded by bonds.

Normally you should invest in preferred stock only if your objective is income, although appreciation is possible if shares are bought at a discount from par or redemption value, or prior to a decline in interest rates. But unless you are a corporation, you probably are better off with a comparable corporate bond, which is less risky in terms of both principal and income.

Invest the Smart Way

*I*n addition to common stocks, you can choose from a number of investment alternatives traded in the securities markets to provide you with the opportunity for capital appreciation, income, or both. But before selecting any investment, you should consider your own particular financial position, risk comfort level, and goals.

CHAPTER 11

Stocks You Can Buy
Direct—Without a Broker

*A*n increasing number of corporations, such as BellSouth, Exxon Corporation, Johnson Controls, Merck, and Texaco, among others, now sell their shares directly to investors through stock purchase and dividend reinvestment plans. For instance, Merck & Company, Inc., a leading research-driven pharmaceutical products and services company, offers its common stock for sale directly through the Merck Stock Investment Plan (800-831-8248), which is administered by Norwest Shareowner Services. The plan is available to investors who do not own Merck stock, as well as to current stockholders, and permits you to make an initial investment of as little as $350. Additional voluntary investments in minimum amounts of $50 can be made as often as weekly, or you can arrange for automatic monthly cash investments. All or a percentage of your dividends may be automatically reinvested in additional shares of Merck common stock.

A similar plan is offered by BellSouth Corporation, a telecommunications company with 1996 revenues of $19 billion and 16 consecutive quarters of improved operating results. The company's direct stock purchase and dividend reinvestment plan permit you to buy and sell BellSouth stock directly. The plan requires an initial investment of at least $500, which includes an enrollment fee of $10. Additional shares can be purchased at any time in minimum amounts of $50. You can reinvest all or part of your cash dividends to accumulate more shares without paying fees.

69

Dividend reinvestment plans, or DRIPs, allow long-term stock market investors who are in the accumulation phase of their investment plans to solve the problem of how to handle income. Dividends received by most individual shareholders are insufficient to buy additional shares economically. And yet, to maximize long-term return, buy-and-hold investors must continuously reinvest investment income. Today, more than 775 companies offer dividend reinvestment plans. A listing of these companies is published annually and may be obtained from the American Association of Individual Investors (312-280-0170).

DRIPs are ideal for buy-and-hold investors and serve as a bonus for shareholders of companies with favorable long-term growth prospects. The plans are simple: Instead of sending cash dividends out to participating investors, the company applies the cash dividends to the purchase of additional shares of company stock.

Participants enjoy several advantages:

- Dividend payments are put to work.
- Transaction costs are eliminated or held to a minimum.
- The additional shares are purchased gradually over time, an effective method of dollar cost averaging (discussed further in Chapter 3).

Special Features

Some company plans have the following special features that make them even more attractive:

- You may make optional cash payments to purchase additional shares through the plan.
- Participants are permitted to receive cash dividends on some of their shares while reinvesting dividends on the remaining shares.
- Shares purchased under the plan are available at discounts ranging from as little as 1 percent to as much as 10 percent.
- Brokerage costs and service fees for share purchases are paid for by the company rather than the participant.

Most DRIPs require that you own shares registered in your name, that is, that you are a shareholder "of record." That means your name must appear on the corporate records as the owner of the shares, rather than having the shares held in "street name" by the broker or bank that may have bought the shares for you and who may be holding them for you. If your shares are held in street name, just ask your broker to transfer the shares to your own name.

Usually, a company will send you a DRIP plan description and an authorization card once you become a registered shareholder. You also can call the company's shareholder relations department or the DRIP agent to request these items. The prospectus or plan description will provide information relating to eligibility requirements, plan options, costs, how and when purchases are made, how and when certificates will be issued, and how you may withdraw from the plan.

How the Plans Work

DRIPs are part of a corporation's overall shareholder relations effort and serve existing shareholders. Some companies, such as utilities, have large investor relations departments and administer their own DRIPs. Most companies, however, hire an outside agent to serve as the administrator for the plan.

The plan administrator maintains records, sends account statements to participants, provides certificates for shares upon request, and liquidates participants' shares when they leave the plan. The agent also has the responsibility of buying company shares for the plan. When you join a plan, you sign a card that authorizes the agent to act on your behalf to purchase shares.

When shares are purchased under a DRIP, they are held by the plan and registered in the nominee name of the agent or plan trustee on behalf of the participants. An account is maintained for each participant under the plan. Most participants hold the company's shares in two places: Your original shares will be held by you or in the custody of a brokerage firm or bank, and the shares purchased through the DRIP will be held by the plan.

Some plans permit participants to deposit certificates of shares registered in their own name into their DRIP account for safekeeping at no cost, or for a small fee. These shares then are treated in the same way as the other shares in the participant's account, making it possible to consolidate all your shares in one safe location.

Certificates for shares purchased under a plan normally are issued only on written request, but often at no charge. Certificates also are issued when a participating shareholder wants to terminate participation.

Options That Are Available

Full reinvestment on all shares of stock registered in the participant's name is standard under the basic DRIP. But under some plans, it is not necessary to reinvest all dividends. Instead, participants may reinvest dividends on a portion of their registered shares, while receiving cash dividends on the remaining shares. This often is referred to as a *partial reinvestment option.*

Many plans permit participants to buy additional shares by making cash payments directly to the plan, sometimes in large allowable amounts. Often referred to as *optional cash payment,* this option offers participants a low-cost way to build a sizable holding in a company. The payments are optional, and participants are not committed to making periodic cash payments. However, there are minimums and usually a maximum for each payment made. Because interest is not paid on payments received in advance, you should find out approximately when the plan invests cash payments it receives.

Some companies also offer a *cash payment only option,* which allows registered shareholders to make cash investments without requiring them to reinvest dividends on the shares they are holding, although they may do so if they wish.

Costs of DRIPs

In general, the cost of participating in a DRIP is low, especially when compared with the alternative of buying shares through a broker.

Service charges and prorated brokerage commissions are the two forms of costs that plan participants may encounter. Service charges cover administrative costs and generally are made on each transaction. Costs can be held down by a participant combining a cash payment with a dividend reinvestment transaction, for charges usually are capped at a maximum of $3 to $5. Brokerage costs paid by the plan when buying shares on the open market are at institutional rates, considerably lower than the rate an individual investor would pay.

Many companies cover all the costs for share purchases from both optional cash payments and reinvested dividends. Some companies assess service charges, others prorate brokerage costs, while still others charge participants for both. The plan prospectus or description spells out which of the many variations apply in your case.

When you terminate participation, some DRIPs will sell plan shares for you if you wish, instead of sending you certificates. The cost to you is usually any prorated brokerage commissions, a lower-cost choice than selling through a broker. Some plans will sell some of your plan share for you, even when you are not terminating. Again, check the prospectus or plan description.

Purchasing Shares

The plan prospectus or description spells out the source of share purchases under a DRIP.

The most common sources are the *secondary market,* a securities exchange where the shares are traded; in the OTC market; or through negotiated transactions. In some cases, the source may be the company itself, using authorized but unissued shares of common stock or shares held in the company's treasury. An advantage to a participant when shares are purchased directly from the company is that there are no brokerage expenses to prorate.

For the company, DRIPs that purchase shares directly from the company provide an inexpensive source of financing. The proceeds often are used for general corporate purposes. From the point of view of investors, however, new issues dilute existing shares, which can have the effect of depressing share prices.

The plan prospectus or description specifies when shares are purchased by the agent. Normally, they coincide with the dividend payment date, but some companies that permit participants to make cash investments have additional investment dates.

When shares are purchased in the open markets, most plans give some discretion to the agent on his or her buying, for a large purchase made on a single date could affect the share price. Usually, the plan requires that all monies be invested within 30 days. The share price for any participant is an average price of all shares purchased for that investment period.

The prospectus or plan description describes how the share price is determined when shares are purchased directly from the company. Generally, it is based on an average of the high and low or the closing price for the stock as reported by a specified source.

Discounts on the share price sometimes are offered to participants in company plans, but with wide variations. In most cases, discounts are available only on shares purchased with reinvested dividends. But some companies permit discounts on shares purchased both with reinvested dividends and with cash payments. A few companies offer discounts only on newly issued corporate shares and not on shares that are bought in the secondary markets.

Taxation and Reinvestment Plans

No special tax advantages are connected with reinvestment plans. A taxable event occurs whether you receive your dividends in cash or have them reinvested. If your dividends are reinvested, the IRS considers the taxable amount to be equal to the fair market value of the shares acquired with the reinvested dividends. That value is the price on the exchange or market where shares are traded, not any discounted price. In addition, any brokerage commissions paid by the company in open market purchases are considered as taxable dividend income to the participant.

At the time shares are sold, the tax basis is the fair market value as of the date the shares were acquired, plus any brokerage commissions paid by the company and treated as income to the participant. If you are a DRIP member, you will receive a Form 1099-DIV each year from the company detailing dividends to be treated as income as reported to the IRS.

Invest the Smart Way

*D*RIPs solve the problem faced by long-term stock market investors of how to handle dividend income. The plans enable buy-and-hold investors to maximize long-term total return by having their dividends automatically reinvested in additional shares of stock, effectively providing an easy-to-implement dollar cost averaging plan.

CHAPTER 12

Ratios the Pros Use

*F*or professional investment analysts and individual investors alike, financial ratios are important tools in the process of selecting stocks for purchase or sale. This chapter explains the principal ratios, what they signify, and how you can use them to increase your success in personal investing.

Ratios indicate relationships, so by themselves, their meaning can be limited and even misleading. Other considerations, such as dollar amount, the overall size of a company, and industry characteristics also are needed in your analysis. Ratios have their greatest significance when used in comparison with industry information or to make year-to-year comparisons to determine trends. Composite ratios for different industries are published by the Federal Trade Commission, Dun & Bradstreet, Standard & Poor's Corporation, and Robert Morris Associates.

To illustrate several commonly used ratios, Figure 12.1 shows a sample summary income statement and balance sheet from an annual report of ABC Corporation in the apparel industry. On December 31 of ABC's fiscal year, the stock traded at $18 per share and paid dividends during the year totaling $.50 per share.

FIGURE 12.1   Sample Abbreviated Income Statement and Balance Sheet

ABC Corporation
Consolidated Statement of Income and Retained Earnings

This statement is a summary of the company's operating performance for one fiscal year. It shows sales and expenses that result in net income. Sales are from the sale of services and products to customers of ABC Corporation. Expenses include costs of services and products; depreciation; and selling, general, and administrative expenses. Taxes are also a major expense category.

Net Income

(Dollars in thousands, except per-share amounts)

	For the year ended December 31, 199X
Net Sales	$346,206
(minus) Cost of Products Sold	(259,344)
Gross Profit	$ 86,862
(minus) Selling, General, and Administrative Expenses	(63,755)
Operating Income	**$ 23,107**
Other Income	$ 3,510
Income Before Taxes	26,617
(Minus Income Taxes)	(10,881)
Net Income	**$ 15,736**
(Plus) Retained Earnings at Beginning of Year	164,263
(Minus) Cash Dividends per Common Share	(7,362)
Retained Earnings at End of Year	$172,637
Net Income per Common Share	$ 1.08

ABC Corporation
Consolidated Balance Sheet

(Dollars in thousands, except per-share amounts)

Assets	December 31, 199X
Current Assets	$146,310
Property, Plant, and Equipment	79,885
Total Assets	**$226,195**
Liabilities and Shareholders' Equity	
Current Liabilities	35,235
Long-Term Debt	1,293
Deferred Income Taxes	3,680
Employee Benefit Plan Liabilities	10,834
Total Liabilities	**51,042**
Shareholders' Equity	
Common Stock, Par Value $.01 per Share, Issued and Outstanding—14,585,800 Shares	146
Retained Earnings	175,007
Total Shareholders' Equity	175,153
Total Liabilities and Shareholders' Equity	**$226,195**

Ratios Used to Measure Stock Values

Price-Earnings (PE) Ratio

This ratio, one of the most widely used and quoted, reflects the value put on a company's earnings and its prospects of future earnings by the securities marketplace. This is important to individual investors because it represents the value of their investments. It also is important from the corporation's point of view because it indicates the price it could expect to receive if it were to issue new shares, that is, its cost of capital.

By itself, a PE ratio may have little meaning. It must be looked at in the context of how it compares with the PE ratios of other companies in the same industry. Over the years and through market cycles, the PE ratio for a particular company can change dramatically. Changes can result from how well or poorly the company is doing, or they may reflect whether the stock market is in a *bull* (upward) or *bear* (downward) trend. At times in the past, a PE ratio of ten times earnings per common share was considered normal for an established company. Earnings per share is calculated by dividing a company's net profits by the total number of common stock shares outstanding. As the stock market has climbed over the past few years, the PE multiple of many companies also has climbed. On March 21, 1997, the PE ratio for the Dow Jones Industrial Average was 18.7 times earnings. The ratio for the Standard & Poor's 500 Composite Stock Index on the same date was 20.3. In the late 1980s, when Japan's Nikkei 225 Stock Index was at its peak, its PE ratio was more than 60 times earnings.

Following is an example of how a PE ratio is calculated for the ABC Corporation, whose common stock is trading at $18 per share and has earnings of $1.08 per share:

$$\frac{\text{Market price of common shares}}{\text{Earnings per common share}} = \frac{18}{1.08} = \begin{array}{c} 16.7 \text{ times earnings} \\ \text{per share} \end{array}$$

ABC Corporation's PE ratio is somewhat higher than average for its industry, which has been running in the range of 12 to 15 times earnings in recent years.

Dividend Payout Ratio

The dividend payout ratio indicates the percentage of earnings per common share that are paid out in dividends. Typically, young companies that are growing rapidly tend to reinvest their earnings to finance expansion, using them as sources of capital so they will have low dividend payout ratios or ratios of zero. Established companies experiencing lower growth rates normally will have higher payout ratios.

In the examples that follow, ABC Corporation has common stock earnings of $1.08 per share and pays out $.50 per share in dividends.

$$\frac{\text{Dividends per common share}}{\text{Earnings per common share}} = \frac{.50}{1.08} = 46.3\%$$

This dividend payout ratio of 46.3 percent by ABC Corporation is higher than typical for most companies in the apparel industry, which have averaged about 25 percent in recent years. In the case of ABC Corporation, its high dividend payout ratio results from a sharp drop in annual earnings without a reduction in the dividend payout.

Market-to-Book Ratio

This ratio indicates the value the market places on the company as a going concern in relation to the value of its shares if the firm were liquidated and the proceeds from the sale of assets, after creditor claims have been satisfied, were paid to shareholders.

$$\frac{\text{Market price of common share}}{\left[\dfrac{\text{Total assets} - \text{Total liabilities}}{\text{Outstanding shares of stock}}\right]} = \frac{18}{12} = 1.5 \text{ times}$$

The market-to-book ratio for ABC Corporation indicates that the market values the company at half again as much as its value would be in liquidation.

Ratios Used to Measure Profitability

Operating Profit Margin

A key to measuring a firm's operating efficiency, this ratio is a reflection on management's purchasing and pricing policies, as well as its success in controlling costs directly associated with running the enterprise and building sales. It does not include other income and expenses, interest, and taxes.

$$\frac{\text{Net operating profit}}{\text{Net sales}} = \frac{23.1}{346.2} = 6.67\%$$

To be useful, the operating profit margin should be compared with how the company has performed in previous years and how it compares with other companies in this industry. ABC's operating profit margin is substantially lower than that of other companies in its industry, which have been about 13 percent. ABC has been going through a difficult competitive environment.

Net Profit Margin

The net profit margin measures management's overall efficiency, not only its success in managing operations but also in terms of borrowing money at favorable rates, investing reserve cash to produce extra income, and taking advantage of tax benefits.

$$\frac{\text{Net income}}{\text{Net sales}} = \frac{15.7}{346.2} = 4.5\%$$

The net profit margin of ABC Corporation is slightly below that of its industry peers, who generally have produced margins averaging just more than 5 percent. In previous years, ABC has enjoyed profit margins in the 8 percent to 10 percent range, well above that of its industry.

Return on Equity

This ratio measures the overall return the company has been able to deliver on shareholder equity. It is the bottom-line profit measured against the money that shareholders have invested in the company.

$$\frac{\text{Net income}}{\text{Total shareholders' equity}} = \frac{15.7}{175.2} = 9.0\%$$

ABC Corporation's return on equity is below average for the apparel industry, reflecting the difficult business conditions it has encountered.

Some other ratios used in analyzing financial statements follow. They are not treated in detail because they are used mainly by professional analysts and by corporate financial officers.

Ratios Used to Measure Liquidity

Ratio		Calculation
Current ratio	=	$\dfrac{\text{Current assets}}{\text{Current liabilities}}$
Quick ratio	=	$\dfrac{\text{Current assets} - \text{inventory}}{\text{Current liabilities}}$

Ratios Used to Measure Activity

Ratio		Calculation
Inventory turnover	=	$\dfrac{\text{Net sales}}{\text{Inventory}}$
Average collection period	=	$\dfrac{\text{Accounts receivable}}{\text{Annual credit sales/360 days}}$
Fixed assets turnover	=	$\dfrac{\text{Net sales}}{\text{Net fixed assets}}$
Total assets turnover	=	$\dfrac{\text{Net sales}}{\text{Total assets}}$

Invest the Smart Way

Ratios can be very helpful to use as a tool in evaluating investment opportunities. By their nature, ratios indicate *relationships* and so must be used in conjunction with other information, such as dollar amounts, size of a company, and industry characteristics. Ratios are most significant when used to make year-to-year comparisons for the purpose of determining trends and comparing industry information.

CHAPTER 13

Buy, Sell, or Hold? Sources to Help You Find the Answers

*I*f you are like most prudent investors, you constantly will seek out securities that you hope will accomplish your objectives. And the best way to do that is to be informed. A host of services, newsletters, and other sources of information is available to investors. Many publications are advertised regularly in *Barron's,* the *Wall Street Journal,* and *Investor's Business Daily.* You can find a complete list of just about all the major publications that can help keep you informed about developments in the world of finance and investment in *The Finance and Investment Handbook* (Barron's Educational Series, Inc., 800-645-3476) by John Downes and Jordan Goodman.

Many of the most popular and useful services are available at your local public library, which is a good place to start and where you can get a feel for which services will be of most value to you. Several of the most useful investment services and organizations are as follows:

American Association of Individual Investors (AAII)
625 North Michigan Avenue
Chicago, IL 60611-3110
312-280-0170

AAII is a not-for-profit corporation recognized under Section 501(C)(3) of the Internal Revenue Code as a public educational organization. Membership in the organization entitles you to the *AAII Journal* (published ten times a year), a tax guide, seminars, study programs, a listing of the major corporations that have dividend reinvestment plans (DRIPs), a stock brokerage survey, and local chapter membership.

Securities Research Company (SRC)
101 Prescott Street
Wellesley Hills, MA 02181
617-235-0900

For investors interested in using technical analysis to predict future price movements, this company produces SRC chart books covering more than 2,100 listed and OTC stocks. Charts plot pure market performance. You get a picture of past price action and how it may repeat or break with prior patterns, resistance levels, turning points, major formations, and volume of buying or selling. All security research charts are plotted on semilogarithmic scales, showing percentage changes rather than ordinary numerical changes.

Standard & Poor's Corporation
25 Broadway
New York, NY 10004
212-208-8000

Standard & Poor's Corporation's highly respected publications cover virtually the full spectrum of investor needs. A partial publications list follows. Some of these publications will be found in your local public library.

Analyst's Handbook	*Growth Stocks Handbook*
Blue List	*High Tech Stocks Handbook*
Bond Guide	*High Yield Quarterly*
Corporation Records	*Income Stocks Handbook*
Daily Action Stock Charts	*OTC Handbook*
Daily Stock Price Record	*Stock Guide*
Dividend Record	*Stock Reports*
Earnings Forecaster	*Stock Summary*

TeleChart 2000 (TC2000) Software Bundle
Worden Brothers, Inc.
4905 Pine Cone Drive
Durham, NC 27707
800-776-4940

TC2000, the number-one selling stock-charting software and data service, is a fully integrated technical analysis service designed to provide an advanced charting module and inexpensive toll-free price data 24 hours a day. This PC up-to-date multicolor charting software provides free daily information on symbol changes, company name changes, stock split dates and ratios, new issues, and so on. TC2000 requires an IBM-PC compatible computer with hard disk, EGA or VGA color monitor, and modem.

The Value Line Investment Survey
711 Third Avenue
New York, NY 10017-4064
800-833-0046

This service provides a complete 2,000-page loose-leaf reference book with full-page reports on all stocks under review.

Every week for each of the 1,700 stocks, *The Value Line Investment Survey* presents the following up-to-date information in its summary and index:

- Rank for probable relative price performance in the next 6 to 12 months, ranging from 1 (highest) down to 5 (lowest)
- Rank for investment safety (from 1 down to 5)
- Estimated yield in the next 12 months
- Estimated appreciation potential in the next three to five years, showing the future "target" price range and the percentage price change indicated
- Current price and estimated price-earnings ratio based on the past six months earnings and estimated annual earnings and dividends in the next 12 months
- The latest available quarterly earnings and dividends, together with year-earlier comparisons

Invest the Smart Way

A host of services, newsletters, and other sources of information is available to investors. Many are advertised regularly in national business publications such as the *Wall Street Journal, Investor's Business Daily,* and *Barron's.* Check with your library for some of the most useful ones. Being informed is one of the best ways to achieve investing success.

CHAPTER 14

Buying Stocks for
Growth—Conservatively

*I*nvestors seeking capital growth generally are most interested in the total return of a stock rather than just the dividends or price appreciation. *Total return* is the sum of the dividend payout per year and the annual change in the market value of the stock. For example, a stock that has a dividend yield of 2 percent and rises 12 percent in value has a total return of 14 percent. The weight you give to dividends when selecting stocks depends on your particular need for income. If growth of capital is your objective, place your emphasis on the sum of annual dividends and price appreciation.

In putting together a portfolio of stocks for growth, it is useful to review the historical record of different categories of stocks. For instance, are you more likely to find success by investing in a group of the largest U.S. companies, or are medium-sized or even small-capitalization companies likely to perform better? The past is not necessarily going to be repeated, but you may get some clues about what to expect. Figure 14.1 illustrates average total returns for one-, three-, five-, and ten-year periods ending March 31, 1997, for three representative market indexes. The S&P 500 is an index of 500 of the largest and most dominant firms in their industries. The S&P MidCap 400 represents the stocks of companies with market capitalizations of between $1 billion and $5 billion. The Russell 2000 is an index of small company stocks with an average market capitalization of about $500 million.

FIGURE 14.1   Average Annual Returns for Periods Ended February 28, 1997

	One Year	Three Years	Five Years	Ten Years
S&P 500 Index	26.15%	22.17%	16.93%	14.17%
S&P MidCap 400 Index	16.92	15.34	13.80	14.34
Russell 2000 Index	12.61	12.49	13.10	10.23

This chapter focuses on financially strong companies that many analysts consider to have above-average potential for long-term price appreciation. In addition to my highlighted company, information is presented on several other companies whose share earnings have increased at a minimum 15 percent average annual rate over the past ten years and are expected to maintain a healthy rate of growth over the next several years. Many growth stocks, including some with better historical and prospective appreciation potential, are not included because of their lower degree of financial strength or the volatility of their price movements. Though all the stocks described in this chapter are high-quality, established companies that have an excellent history, I strongly recommend that your stock portfolio be diversified among at least ten companies to effectively eliminate company risk.

A Recommended Company

Merck & Company, Inc., is a good example of a stock that may be considered for growth in a conservative portfolio. It is a financially strong company that has performed very well over many years and has a bright outlook for the future. New products are likely to drive earnings expansion through the 1990s and beyond.

Merck & Company, Inc.

P.O. Box 100
Whitehouse Station, NJ 08889-0100
908-423-2001   800-613-2104

Chairman, president, and CEO: Raymond V. Gilmartin
Number of shareholders: 243,000
Number of employees: 45,200
Where the stock trades: NYSE
Symbol: MRK

What the Company Does

Merck is a leading manufacturer of human and animal health care products and specialty chemical products. Important product names include Vasotec, Prinvil (angiotensin converting enzyme (ACE) inhibitor agents for high blood pressure and angina); Mevacor, Zocor (cholesterol-lowering agents); Fosamax (osteoporosis); Pepcid (anti-ulcer agent); Recombivax HB (hepatitis B vaccine); and Prilosec (gastrointestinal).

International business accounts for 30 percent of sales and 28 percent of pretax profits. Investment in research and development represents about 8 percent of sales.

Recent Financial History of Merck & Company

Over the past 15 years, sales per share of Merck & Company, Inc., have experienced an uninterrupted increase each year. Earnings per share have kept pace, rising from 30 cents in 1981 to $3.20 in 1996, showing an increase each and every year. Dividends have also grown steadily, from 14 cents a share in 1981 to $1.42 in 1996. The company typically has paid out about 45 percent of its profits in dividends. If you had invested $10,000 in Merck shares in 1985 (at the average price the stock traded at during the year), with dividends reinvested each year in additional shares, by the end of 1996 you would have owned 2,065 shares with a value of $164,425. Brokerage commissions and taxes have not been considered. Figure 14.2 shows the 12 years' results of a $10,000 investment in Merck common stock from 1985 to 1996. All numbers have been adjusted for stock splits in 1986, 1988, and 1992.

The December 31, 1996, closing price of Merck & Company common stock shares on the NYSE was 79⅝. At the end of 12 years, the original $10,000 investment had a market value of $164,425, which included reinvested dividends of $16,343. Dividends of $2,875 paid in 1996 represented an effective yield on the original investment of more than 28 percent. The value of the $10,000 investment had multiplied by more than 16 times.

FIGURE 14.2   Results of a $10,000 Investment in Merck & Company, Inc., Common Stock in 1985 (Adjusted for Stock Splits)

	Average Share Price	Annual Dividends	Shares Bought from Dividends	Total Shares Owned	Average Value in Year
1985	$ 6.35	$ 283	44	1,618	$ 10,278
1986	10.95	340	31	1,649	18,056
1987	19.20	445	23	1,672	32,106
1988	17.95	719	40	1,712	30,731
1989	22.85	942	41	1,753	40,060
1990	26.35	1,122	42	1,795	47,313
1991	41.50	1,382	33	1,828	75,875
1992	48.60	1,682	34	1,862	90,519
1993	36.35	1,918	52	1,914	69,602
1994	33.80	2,182	64	1,978	66,875
1995	51.85	2,453	47	2,025	105,012
1996	70.38	2,875	40	2,065	145,394

Note: Merck & Company has a dividend reinvestment plan (DRIP).

Two interesting aspects of an investment in Merck can be seen in Figure 14.2. First, while the stock price did not pursue a continual upward move (the average price dipped in 1988, 1993, and 1994), a patient investor benefited in those years because dividends bought more shares at lower prices than at higher prices. Second, the company increased its dividend payout every year.

Merck has been able to produce an unbroken and increasing stream of profits for its shareholders. The average PE ratio for Merck has varied over the 12-year period from as low as 14 times earnings in 1994 to as high as 25 times earnings in 1987. In early 1997 the PE multiple was up to 27 times earnings. A high PE ratio indicates investor bullishness about a stock.

Excessive optimism can lead to a price correction, both in a particular security and in the market as a whole. In early 1997, the median of estimated PE ratios of all stocks included in the S&P 500 index was 19 times earnings. Shortly before the October 19, 1987, market collapse, the market hit a high on September 4. The PE ratio on that day was 16.9. On December 23, 1974, at the bottom of the 1973–1974 bear market, the PE ratio was 4.8! A high PE ratio may be a signal that a correction is near.

FIGURE 14.3   Companies for Consideration in a Conservative Growth Portfolio

Company	Ticker Symbol	Price-Earnings Ratio April 4, 1997	April 4, 1997 Stock Price
American International Group, Inc.	AIG	19	115½
Automatic Data Processing, Inc.	AUD	26	43⅛
The Coca-Cola Company	KO	41	57⅜
The Walt Disney Company	DIS	35	73¾
The Gillette Company	G	44	78
The Home Depot, Inc.	HD	28	54⅝
The Interpublic Group of Companies	IPG	21	54¾
Johnson & Johnson	JNJ	25	54⅝
Microsoft Corporation	MSFT	49	94⅜

Creating a Conservative Growth Stock Portfolio

To eliminate the risk that comes from investing all your money in one stock, hold at least ten stocks in your investment portfolio. Seek the stocks of financially strong companies that have solid records of earnings growth and that are expected to continue to increase their earnings at above-average rates. Invest in companies whose share earnings have grown at a minimum average annual rate of at least 10 percent in recent years and can be expected to continue that performance in future years. For conservative investment portfolios, companies should exhibit characteristics of safety and good price stability.

Information on a number of top-quality companies that meet these criteria is shown in Figure 14.3. The shares of these stocks are all traded on the NYSE, with the exception of Microsoft, which is traded on the Nasdaq. They are typical of companies that prudent investors would want for a small portfolio of growth stocks with low risk. All numbers have been adjusted for stock splits. You can receive earnings reports and other information about these companies by calling the telephone numbers provided in the next section and asking for the investor relations department.

Many growth stocks have had better past performance and appear to have a bright potential for the future, but are not included in this list because of their less-than-favorable financial positions or their volatile share price movements.

What the Companies Do

American International Group, Inc. (212-770-7000). American International is a holding company. Domestic property and casualty insurance operations rank fourth in the United States based on premiums written. The company also sells individual and group life and health insurance and provides risk management and agency services. Foreign operations account for about 50 percent of total revenues, which exceed $12 billion. Per-share earnings rose from 87 cents in 1985 to $6.15 in 1996. The stock price increased tenfold during the same period.

Automatic Data Processing, Inc. (ADP) (201-994-5000). The nation's largest payroll and tax filing processor, ADP has 300,000 accounts, which account for about 55 percent of the company's total revenues of more than $3.5 billion. Brokerage services provide front-office quotation workstations and back-office recordkeeping, order entry, and proxy services for brokerage firms. ADP also provides specialized services for auto and truck dealerships. From 1985 to 1996, earnings per share rose from 31 cents to $1.57, while the stock price increased more than 700 percent.

The Coca-Cola Company. (404-676-2121). The world's largest soft drink company, Coca-Cola distributes major brands (Coca-Cola, Sprite, Fanta, TAB, etc.) through bottlers throughout the world. Foreign operations account for more than 70 percent of sales and 80 percent of profits. Revenues total in excess of $19 billion. Earnings per share have increased from 22 cents in 1985 to $1.40 in 1996. The share price increased by a multiple of 19 during the period.

The Walt Disney Company. (818-560-1000). The Disney Company operates Disneyland and Walt Disney World; supplies entertainment for theaters, TV, and video; licenses rights; publishes books; and records music. Foreign sales account for about 20 percent of revenues, which total more than $20 billion. Earnings per share have grown from 32 cents in 1985 to $1.96 in 1996, while the stock price rose by a multiple of 14.

The Gillette Company. (617-421-7000). Gillette is a leading producer of grooming aids. Its major divisions include razors, toiletries, stationery products, oral care, and Braun. Foreign operations account for about 70 percent of sales and 65 percent of earnings. Total sales exceed $7.5 billion. Earnings per share rose from 32 cents in 1985 to $1.71 in 1996. The market price per share rose 1,200 percent during that period.

The Home Depot, Inc. (404-433-8211). Home Depot operates a chain of retail building supply/home improvement warehouse stores in 28 U.S. states and three Canadian provinces. Product lines include building materials; lumber, flooring, and wall coverings; plumbing, heating, and electrical supplies; paint and furniture; seasonal and specialty items; hardware and tools. Earnings per share rose from 3 cents in 1985 to $1.94 in 1996. The share price grew during that period from $2 to $54.

The Interpublic Group of Companies. (212-399-8000). The Interpublic Group is the second largest organization of advertising agencies in the world, serving more than 4,000 clients through 400 offices in 100 countries. Foreign operations account for more than 60 percent of revenues and profits. Its three largest clients are Unilever, General Motors, and Coca-Cola. Earnings increased from 56 cents in 1985 to $2.56 in 1996. The common shares rose during that period by 800 percent.

Johnson & Johnson. (908-524-0400). A leading manufacturer of health-care products, Johnson & Johnson's segments are consumer, professional, and pharmaceutical. Well-known brands include Tylenol, Band-Aid, Stayfree, Modess, and Reach. Foreign business accounts for more than half of sales. Earnings per share have increased from 42 cents in 1985 to $2.17 in 1996. The share price increased by a factor of nine during the period.

Microsoft Corporation. (206-882-8080). Microsoft is the world's largest independent maker of personal computer software. Revenue from platforms accounts for about 40 percent of revenue and is derived from sales of Windows 95, MS-DOS, Windows, and LAN Manager. Applications and content revenue (60 percent of revenue) is derived from sales of word processing, spreadsheet, office suites, and other business programs. Earnings per share grew from 5 cents in 1986 to $3.40 in 1996. The share price at the end of 1996 was approximately 95 times that of the 1986 price.

Invest the Smart Way

One of the oldest and most popular investment approaches involves finding companies expected to have above-average rates of earnings growth. This "growth stock" strategy assumes that, over time, the price of a company's stock will reflect its earnings. For successful growth stock investing, focus on well-managed companies whose earnings and dividends are expected to grow faster than both inflation and the overall economy.

CHAPTER 15

Buying Stocks for Growth—Aggressively

*A*ll investments involve risk. Aggressive investing generally means more risk. The important thing to remember is that the return you expect should correlate to the risk you expose yourself to. An investor willing to take on a higher degree of risk should expect a higher return on money invested. To properly manage your investment portfolio, decide in advance on the degree of risk you are prepared to accept.

The price sensitivity of a stock to market changes is measured by its *beta*. Beta measures this sensitivity with values above and below 1.00. Any value above 1.00 indicates that a stock price tends to move more than the market. For instance, a stock with a beta of 1.10 tends to move 10 percent more than the market as a whole. A stock with a high beta can be expected to post larger-than-average declines when the market is falling and higher-than-average returns in a rising market. On the other hand, stocks with betas below 1.00 would tend to have price changes that fluctuate less than the general market. So low beta stocks typically realize below-average returns in a bull market and smaller-than-average declines during a bear market. A stock with a beta of 1.00 would be expected to have price changes that fluctuate about the same as the market.

The beta of stocks included in an aggressive growth portfolio are normally on the high side. For instance, the beta of Microsoft Corporation is 1.2, so its price changes should fluctuate about 20 percent more than the market as a whole.

If your investment objective is capital appreciation and you want to pursue your objective aggressively, be prepared for a certain amount of risk. Diversify your portfolio into at least ten stocks to effectively eliminate company risk, the risk in owning just one stock. Following my highlighted stock are a number of other well-regarded companies whose stocks are expected to have superior performance in the next five to ten years. Most of these companies are young and tend to be highly volatile.

A Recommended Company

Oracle Corporation is a company whose stock I recommend for inclusion in an aggressive growth portfolio. It is a good example of a company of average financial strength that has performed very well over recent years and that has a bright outlook for the future. Oracle's products have continued to be strong, both for database products and applications. Solid gains appear to be in the cards for the next several years, at least. If you are able to tolerate Oracle stock's high degree of volatility, a long-term investment should prove very rewarding.

Oracle Corporation

500 Oracle Parkway
Redwood City, CA 94065
415-506-7000

Chairman and CEO: Lawrence J. Ellison
Number of shareholders: 3,950
Number of employees: 25,000
Where the stock trades: Nasdaq
Symbol: ORCL

What the Company Does

Oracle Corporation is the world's largest seller of database software and information management services. The company's software runs on almost every computer, from the smallest laptop to the largest massively parallel computer, and is used to manage everything from personal information to giant corporations. It allows users to create, retrieve, and manipulate data in computer-based files. Products include the Oracle7 Universal Server, a complete suite of developer tools, and an integrated family of application products.

Foreign sales account for nearly 60 percent of Oracle's total revenues and a similar percent of profits. About 9 percent of sales is invested in research and development.

Recent Financial History of Oracle Corporation

Since 1986, sales of Oracle have grown from $55 million to more than $4 billion in 1996. Earnings per share, 1 cent in 1986, grew to 90 cents in 1996. Earnings increased every year except for 1991, when the company posted a loss of 2 cents a share. Oracle has never paid a dividend; all earnings have been reinvested back in the business. The company's stock has risen from less than $1 a share in 1986 (adjusted for stock splits in 1986, 1987, 1989, 1993, 1995, and 1996) to 41¾ at the end of 1996. An investment of $10,000 at the average share price in 1986 would have been worth more than $600,000 in 1996. Figure 15.1 shows the 11 years' results of a $10,000 investment in Oracle Corporation common stock from 1986 to 1996.

The stock price of Oracle Corporation did not pursue a continual upward course. As a result of a business slump, the average price of the stock dropped in 1990 and again in 1991. The stock was highly volatile during the 11-year period. In 1989 the stock traded as high as 5⅞ and as low as 2⅛. Then in 1990, the high was 6⅜ and the low was 1⅛. Wide share price swings of this stock have occurred in most years. Volatility can work to your advantage or disadvantage. Courageous investors who take advantage of price drops can add to their holdings at low prices. On the other hand, nervous investors may sell out when they experience lower prices, only to miss out on future price appreciation.

Creating an Aggressive Growth Stock Portfolio

As in all stock investing, to effectively eliminate company risk, hold at least ten stocks in your aggressive growth portfolio. Seek stocks of companies that have solid records of earnings growth and that are expected to continue to increase their earnings at above-average rates. Invest in companies whose share earnings have grown at a minimum

FIGURE 15.1   Results of a $10,000 Investment in Oracle Corporation
Common Stock in 1986 (Adjusted for Stock Splits)

	Average Share Price*	Average Value During the Year	Earnings per Share	Average PE Ratio
1986	.60	$ 10,000	$.01	60
1987	1.35	22,499	.03	45
1988	1.90	31,665	.07	27
1989	3.95	65,830	.14	28
1990	3.70	61,664	.19	19
1991	2.45	40,831	d.02	N/A
1992	4.55	75,830	.10	46
1993	11.35	189,159	.24	47
1994	16.20	269,989	.43	38
1995	25.15	419,149	.67	38
1996	36.69	611,475	.95	39

*All numbers are adjusted for stock splits in 1986, 1987, 1989, 1993, 1995, and 1996.
d—Deficit

average annual rate of at least 15 percent in recent years and that can be expected to continue that performance in the future. Typically, such companies do not pay dividends. Rather, earnings are reinvested to help finance future growth.

Information on a few highly regarded companies that meet these criteria is listed in Figure 15.2. Shares of these stocks trade on the NYSE or the Nasdaq market. They are typical of companies that investors who are willing to take prudent risks would consider for a small portfolio of growth stocks that have superior potential for price appreciation. All numbers shown have been adjusted for stock splits. You can receive earnings reports and other information about any of these companies by calling the telephone number provided and asking for the company's investor relations department.

Because the share price movement of such companies can be quite volatile, you should carefully consider the amount of risk you are able to tolerate. Diversifying your assets into the shares of a number of companies helps to reduce your risk exposure. Many excellent, fast-growing companies are not included in the list in Figure 15.2. You can get detailed information on many of them by consulting an investment resource like *The Value Line Investment Survey,* which probably is available in your public library.

FIGURE 15.2 Companies for Consideration in an Aggressive
Growth Portfolio

Company	Ticker Symbol	Where Traded	April 4, 1997 PE Ratio	April 4, 1997 Stock Price
America Online	AOL	NYSE	96	48⅜
BMC Software	BMCS	Nasdaq	35	49⅜
Cisco Systems, Inc.	CSCO	Nasdaq	33	50⅞
Compaq Computer Corporation	CPQ	NYSE	16	76
Intel Corporation	INTC	Nasdaq	25	145
Linear Technology Corporation	LLTC	Nasdaq	30	50⅛
3Com Corporation	COMS	Nasdaq	20	34⅜

What the Companies Do

America Online, Inc.   (703-448-8700). This leading provider
of online information services for personal computers has more than
six million subscribers. It offers electronic mail and conferencing,
online forums and classes, interactive newspapers and magazines, and
access to the Internet. From its initial public offering in 1992 to 1996,
sales increased from $26 million to more than $1 billion and earnings
per share rose from 5 cents to 50 cents. The stock rose from an average
price of $2.50 in 1992 to $48 in early 1997.

BMC Software, Inc.   (713-918-8800). BMC develops, markets, and supports data and application management software targeted
at IBM's database and data communication systems (mainframes) and
the open-systems computing environment. Foreign operations
accounts for 42 percent of sales. About 14 percent of sales is invested
in research and development. From its initial public offering in 1988
through 1996, sales increased from $60 million to more than $560 million and earnings per share rose from 4 cents to $1.53. The stock rose
from an average price of $1.83 in 1988 to $49 in early 1997.

Cisco Systems, Inc.   (408-526-4000). Cisco is the leading supplier of high-performance internetworking products for linking local-
area and wide-area networks of computer systems. Products include
routers, LAN and ATM switches, deal-up access servers, and network

management software. From its initial public offering in 1990 through 1996, sales increased from $70 million to $4 billion and earnings per share rose from 3 cents to $1.40. The stock rose from an average price of $1.00 in 1990 to $50 in early 1997.

Compaq Computer Corporation. (713-370-0670). Compaq produces laptop and desktop personal computers that are IBM compatible. The company is a leading player in the market for portable computers and PC servers and has a leading share of the IBM-compatible desktop market. Products are sold through mail order and 38,000 outlets worldwide. From 1986 to 1996, sales increased from $625 million to $19 billion and earnings per share rose from 22 cents to $4.72. The stock rose from an average price of $2.75 in 1986 to $76 in early 1997.

Intel Corporation. (408-765-8080). Intel is a leading manufacturer of integrated circuits, serving makers of personal computers, communications, industrial automation, military, and other electronic equipment. Its main products include microprocessors, microcontrollers, and memory chips. From 1986 to 1996, sales increased from $1.2 billion to $20 billion and earnings per share rose from a deficit of 26 cents to a profit of $5.81. The stock rose from an average price of $4.05 in 1986 to $145 in early 1997.

Linear Technology Corporation. (408-432-1900). This company designs, manufactures, and markets analog (also called linear) integrated circuits. These circuits monitor, condition, amplify, or transform continuous analog signals associated real-world phenomena (such as temperature, pressure, weight, position, light, sound, or speed). From its initial public offering in 1986 through 1996, sales increased from $22 million to $370 million and earnings per share rose from 2 cents to $1.70. The stock rose from an average price of $1.95 in 1986 to $50 in early 1997.

3Com Corporation. (408-764-5000). 3Com designs, manufactures, markets, and services networking products for a global clientele. Products include network adapters, routers, hubs, switches, network management, communications servers, and protocols. From 1986 to 1996, sales increased from $64 million to $2 billion and earnings per share rose from 12 cents to $1.58. The stock rose from an average price of $3.15 in 1986 to $34 in early 1997.

Invest the Smart Way

The return you expect from aggressive investing should correlate to the risk you are able to accept. If you are willing to take on a higher degree of risk, you should expect a higher return on your money invested. The type of stocks described in this chapter tends to be highly volatile, so diversify your aggressive growth portfolio into at least ten stocks to reduce company risk, the risk you would have if you owned just one stock.

CHAPTER 16

Buying Stocks for a Growing Income

*I*nvestors who seek current income that gradually will grow over the years as a way to offset the ravages of persistent inflation can easily put together a portfolio of common stocks that have a history of consistent dividend increases and that are expected to maintain the pattern in the future.

In early 1997, the median of estimated yields for all dividend-paying common stocks was about 2.1 percent, according to *The Value Line Investment Survey*. This yield is near the bottom of what stocks have paid in recent years. On December 23, 1974, when stocks were at a bear market low, the dividend yield was 7.8 percent. On September 4, 1987, just before the 1987 bear market began, dividends yielded 2.3 percent.

Though it is true that stocks as a whole were yielding about 2 percent in early 1997, some segments of the market were yielding much more. For instance, the electric utility and real estate investment trust sectors were yielding about 6 percent. When seeking income that will increase over the years, it is important to differentiate between stocks. I recommend that you focus on companies with a history of consistent earnings growth. Avoid buying stocks on a yield basis alone, as an abnormally high dividend rate is usually a sign of impaired growth prospects, or perhaps an imminent payout reduction. Generally, there is an inverse relationship between a high dividend payout and future growth. The higher the dividend, the less earnings a company has available to grow the business.

It is rarely possible, except by luck, to pinpoint when the market or the price of a particular stock has reached even a temporary high or low point. Many investors solve the problem of determining the best time to invest in common stocks by using the principle of *dollar cost averaging,* investing a constant number of dollars at regular intervals. (See Chapter 3 for a full discussion of this important concept.)

You can put together a portfolio of stocks that will produce a regular income, with an expectation that the income gradually will grow through annual dividend increases, while at the same time your investment will increase in value. To do this, buy common stocks of high-quality, established companies that have a history of increasing their dividends on a regular basis over the years. This chapter highlights and gives historical data of one such corporation, Weingarten Realty Investors, that appears to fulfill these criteria. Because diversification is desirable to effectively eliminate the problem of *company risk* (the risk of owning just one stock), I have also provided information on a number of other solid dividend-paying companies to consider for your portfolio.

A Recommended Company

Weingarten Realty Investors is a good example of a company that pays a competitive yield and has a history of consistently increasing its dividend over the years. In early 1997 the stock was trading at $42 a share and paying quarterly dividends of 64 cents a share ($2.56 annually), producing a yield of 6.1 percent.

Weingarten Realty Investors

P.O. Box 924133
Houston, TX 77292
713-866-6000

Chairman and CEO: Stanford Alexander
Number of shareholders: 2,600
Where the stock trades: NYSE
Symbol: WRI

What the Company Does

Weingarten Realty Investors is a regional real estate investment trust that emphasizes the acquisition, development, and long-term ownership of anchored shopping centers. The company has a portfolio of 175 properties. These include 155 shopping centers, 17 industrial properties, two multi-family residential properties, and one office building. Holdings are concentrated in the greater Houston area, Texas, and in ten states throughout the Southwest.

Recent Financial History of Weingarten Realty Investors

Rental income of Weingarten Realty increased from $49 million in 1986 to $145 million in 1996. Earnings per share also grew, rising from $1.26 in 1986 to $1.80 in 1996. Dividends rose gradually from $1.56 a share in 1986 to $2.48 in 1996. The company typically has paid out about 80 percent of its profits in dividends.

If you had invested $10,000 in Weingarten Realty Investors in 1986 (at the average price the stock traded at during the year), you would have bought 449 shares. With dividends reinvested each year in additional shares, by the end of 1996 (when the share price was 40⅝) you would have owned 892 shares with a value of $36,237. Dividends of $2,137 paid in 1996 on the total shares owned represented a yield of more than 21 percent on your original investment. Brokerage commissions and taxes have not been considered.

Figure 16.1 shows the 11 years' results of a $10,000 investment in Weingarten Realty common stock from 1986 to 1996 with dividends reinvested in additional shares.

If dividends had not been reinvested, your original $10,000 investment would have had a market value of $18,240 at the end of 1996 (at the 40⅝ closing price). Dividends of $1,149 paid in 1996 on the original 449 shares represented an effective yield on the $10,000 investment of nearly 11.5 percent, growing from the 1986 yield of 7 percent. In addition, the value of the $10,000 investment had nearly doubled.

FIGURE 16.1 Results of a $10,000 Investment in Weingarten Realty Investors Common Stock in 1986 with Dividends Reinvested

	Average Share Price	Annual Dividends	Shares Bought from Dividends	Total Shares Owned	Average Value in Year
1986	22.25	700	31	480	10,680
1987	23.45	768	32	512	12,006
1988	25.35	860	34	546	13,841
1989	28.85	961	33	579	16,704
1990	27.05	1,088	40	619	16,744
1991	28.50	1,188	41	660	18,810
1992	33.75	1,376	40	700	23,625
1993	40.90	1,512	37	737	30,143
1994	36.65	1,680	45	783	28,696
1995	35.95	1,879	52	835	30,018
1996	37.50	2,137	57	892	33,450

Note: Weingarten Realty Investors has a dividend reinvestment plan.

Creating a Portfolio of Stocks with Increasing Dividend Potential

Following are some guidelines for building a portfolio of dividend-paying stocks with the potential for increasing returns:

- Hold at least ten stocks in your portfolio, to eliminate the risk that comes from investing all your money in one stock.
- Seek the stocks of financially strong companies that have solid records of earnings growth and that are expected to continue to increase their dividends at above-average rates.
- For conservative investment portfolios, the stocks you select should exhibit characteristics of safety and good price stability.
- Look for stocks whose yields from dividend payouts generally are higher than those of most other dividend-paying companies and where the company's payout ratio is generous. A firm's *payout ratio* is the company's dividends as a percentage of its net profit.

FIGURE 16.2 Stocks Expected to Provide a Stream of Growing Dividends

Company	Symbol	Where Traded	4/18/97 Stock Price	Percent Yield
ARCO Chemical Company	RCM	NYSE	42	6.7%
Baltimore Gas and Electric Company	BGE	NYSE	25¾	6.2
Boston Edison Company	BSE	NYSE	25⅝	7.3
British Telecommunications, PLC	BTY	NYSE	72¾	5.2
Buckeye Partners, L.P.	BPL	NYSE	42⅛	7.1
Carolina Power and Light Company	CPL	NYSE	35⅛	5.4
Cedar Fair, L.P.	FUN	NYSE	39¼	6.4
Duke Power Company	DUK	NYSE	43¼	4.9
Hong Kong Telecommunications, Ltd.	HKT	NYSE	16⅞	5.5

Listed in Figure 16.2 is information on a number of top-quality companies that meet these criteria. They are typical of companies that prudent investors could include in a portfolio of high dividend–paying stocks with low risk. You can receive earnings reports and other information about these companies by calling the telephone number provided in the next section and asking for the investor relations department.

What the Companies Do

ARCO Chemical Company. (610-359-2000). ARCO is a leading multinational manufacturer of chemicals. Nearly half its sales are derived from Europe and Asia Pacific. Total revenues grew from $1.5 billion in 1986 to $3.5 billion in 1996. Dividends per share paid during the period increased from $1.44 to $2.80. The company has typically paid out about 80 percent of earnings in dividends. The stock price was at about the same level in early 1997 as its initial public offering in 1987.

Baltimore Gas and Electric Company.   (410-783-5920).
This company sells electricity and gas throughout central Maryland to
a population of approximately 2.5 million people. Electric revenues account for about 75 percent of total sales of $3 billion. Revenues grew
from $1.8 billion in 1986 to $3.1 billion in 1996. Dividends paid per
share increased from $1.19 in 1986 to $1.60 in 1996. The company has
typically paid out about 80 percent of earnings in dividends. The stock
price rose from an average of $15 in 1986 to an average of $28 in 1996.

Boston Edison Company.   (617-424-2000). Boston Edison
supplies electricity to an area of approximately 590 square miles in
eastern Massachusetts, encompassing Boston and 39 surrounding
towns and cities. The company serves about 650,000 customers. Revenues have grown from $1.1 billion in 1986 to $1.6 billion in 1996. Dividends paid per share increased from $1.75 in 1986 to $1.88 in 1996.
The company has typically paid out about 80 percent of earnings in dividends. The average stock price was $25 in 1986 and $26 in 1996.

British Telecommunications, PLC.   (800-331-4568). The
principal supplier of telecommunications services in the United Kingdom, British Telecommunications has a market share of 83 percent of
business calls and 93 percent of residential calls. Revenues grew from
$15 billion in 1986 to $29 billion in 1996. Dividends paid per American depositary receipt (ADR) share increased from $1.86 in 1986 to
$3.82 in 1996. (For more information on ADRs, see Chapter 17.) The
company has typically paid out about 60 percent of earnings in dividends. The stock (ADR) price rose from an average of $34 in 1986 to
an average of $59 in 1996.

Buckeye Partners, L.P.   (610-770-4000). Buckeye Partners is
a master limited partnership engaged primarily in the transportation of
refined petroleum products including gasoline, jet fuel, and distillates.
The principal operating entity is Buckeye Pipe Line Company. Most of
the partnership's distributions paid to shareholders are tax-deferred.
Distributions per share increased from $1.65 in 1987 to $3.00 in 1996.
The company has typically paid out about 80 percent of earnings in dividends. The stock price rose from its original offering price of $20 in
1986 to an average of $38 in 1996.

Carolina Power and Light Company.   (919-546-7474). This company supplies electricity to portions of North Carolina and South Carolina. Dividends per share increased from $1.35 in 1986 to $1.84 in 1996. The company has typically paid out about 75 percent of earnings in dividends. The stock price rose from an average of $18 in 1986 to an average of $36 in 1996.

Cedar Fair, L.P.   (419-626-0830). This master limited partnership is managed by Cedar Fair Management Company. It owns and operates four amusement/theme parks, one each in Ohio, Minnesota, Pennsylvania, and Missouri. The partnership is not subject to corporate taxation. Distributions per share increased from $.71 in 1987 (the year of its initial public offering) to $2.50 in 1996. The company has typically paid out about 80 percent of earnings in distributions. The stock price rose from its original offering price of $12 in 1987 to an average of $35 in 1996.

Duke Power Company.   (704-594-0887). This company supplies electricity to 1.7 million customers in the Piedmont section of North and South Carolina. Total revenues are derived as follows: residential, 33 percent; commercial, 24 percent; and industrial, 28 percent, with the balance coming from other sources. Revenues grew from $3.4 billion in 1986 to $4.7 billion in 1996. Dividends paid per share increased from $1.32 in 1986 to $2.12 in 1996. The company typically has paid out about 70 percent of earnings in dividends. The stock price rose from an average of $22 in 1986 to an average of $48 in 1996.

Hong Kong Telecommunications, Ltd.   (212-593-4813). This company has exclusive franchises for international telecommunications services in Hong Kong to the year 2006. The company has 3.1 million lines in service (67 per 100 inhabitants). One hundred percent of its lines are digital. Revenues increased from $1 billion in 1986 to $4 billion in 1996. Dividends paid per ADR share increased from 29 cents in 1988 (the year shares began trading) to 92 cents in 1996. The company has typically paid out about 75 percent of earnings in dividends. The price of the ADR shares rose from an average of $7 in 1986 to an average of $18 in 1996.

Invest the Smart Way

*I*f you are seeking a current income that gradually will grow over the years as a way to offset inflation, assemble a portfolio of common stocks that have a history of consistent dividend increases and are expected to maintain that pattern in the future. But remember, the higher the percentage of profits a company pays out in dividends, the lower should be your expectation for future earnings and dividend growth.

CHAPTER 17

Investing in
Stocks Worldwide

*I*f you already have a well-rounded portfolio of domestic stocks, then diversifying with international investments can be a wise decision. The U.S. market now accounts for about only 40 percent of the world's total stock market value. So if you restrict yourself to that market, you ignore the growth potential of the other two-thirds, located mainly in Europe and Asia. An individual investor easily can buy shares in many companies headquartered outside the United States without dealing directly with foreign exchanges.

Investors seeking foreign-domiciled company investments can buy American depositary receipts (ADRs) in U.S. markets, instead of buying shares in overseas markets. ADRs are traded on the NYSE, the AMEX, and the OTC market. They are also called *American depositary shares.*

Invented in 1927 by J.P. Morgan, ADRs are receipts for the shares of foreign-based corporations; they are held in American bank vaults. Three American banks—the Bank of New York, Citibank, and J.P. Morgan—are the major depository institutions for ADRs. They provide custody of the foreign shares, change dividends into dollars, and help distribute company reports.

The owner of an ADR in the United States is entitled to the same dividends and capital gains accruing to a shareholder who purchases shares on an exchange in the home country of the company. Each ADR represents a specified number of common shares of the company it represents. Quoted prices reflect the latest currency exchange rates, for

ADRs are denominated in U.S. dollars. Prices of ADRs are reported in the stock listings of the *New York Times,* the *Wall Street Journal,* and other newspapers, as well as in electronic databases.

Foreign corporations with ADRs normally are well-established and financially stable companies with worldwide operations. In many cases, you will be familiar with them because their products and services are offered in the United States. Altogether, more than 1,000 ADRs are traded on American exchanges and the Nasdaq, with new ADRs added each month. More than 250 trade on the NYSE and the AMEX. For a complete list of ADRs and how they work, see *The McGraw-Hill Handbook of American Depositary Receipts,* McGraw-Hill, Monterey Avenue, Blue Ridge Summit, PA 17294; ($59.95) 800-722-4726.

ADRs with Potential for Growth and Income

In selecting shares of foreign corporations, evaluate ADRs the same way you would shares of U.S. companies, considering such issues as your personal investment objective, the relative safety of the company, and whether the timing is right in terms of the particular industry and company. If you own mutual funds, a simple way to see what the pros are buying is to check your mutual fund annual report and see what its largest international holdings are. You also can find the same information contained in the reports on foreign mutual funds published in *Morningstar Mutual Funds* and *The Value Line Mutual Fund Survey.* You are likely to find one or both of these publications in your public library.

One industry that appears to give investors in ADRs potential for long-term capital appreciation and increasing dividends is *telecommunications.* The following telecommunications company exhibits the relative safety and timeliness that prudent investors look for.

A Recommended Company

Reuters Holdings PLC was formerly controlled by three associations representing publishers in Britain, Australia, and New Zealand. It went public on June 4, 1984, when the publishers and the company sold a total of 214 million shares. Of these, 26 million American depositary receipts (representing 78 million shares) were sold in the United States at $4.125 each (adjusted for splits in 1988 and 1994). The founder's share, administered by trustees, has voting control to ensure that Reuters maintains its independence, and that no group controls 30 percent or more of the shares.

Reuters Holdings PLC

U.S. Address
1700 Broadway
New York, NY 10019
212-603-3500

CEO: Peter Job. *Chairman:* Sir Christopher Hogg
Number of shareholders: 17,000
Number of employees: 14,180
Where the ADRs trade: Nasdaq
Symbol: RTRSY

What the Company Does

Reuters Holdings PLC, is the leading supplier of real-time information systems and automated trading services to the financial community worldwide. The company is also the world's largest electronic publisher. Information systems produce 69 percent of total revenues, 25 percent comes from transaction services, and media operations account for the balance.

Europe, the Middle East, and Africa account for 55 percent of total sales; 18 percent comes from the Asia/Pacific region; 15 percent from North and South America; and 9 percent from Instinet.

Recent Financial History of Reuters Holdings, PLC

Over the years since 1986, revenues per ADR of Reuters have experienced nearly uninterrupted growth, increasing in every year except 1992. Earnings per ADR have kept pace, rising from 41 cents in 1986 to $3.10 in 1996, showing an increase each year but 1992. Dividends have also grown steadily, from 17 cents a share in 1986 to $1.17 in 1996. The company typically has paid out about 40 percent of its profits in dividends. If you had invested $10,000 in Reuters ADRs in 1986 (at the average price the stock traded at during the year), with dividends reinvested each year in additional shares, by the end of 1996 you would have owned 1,226 shares with a value of $80,916. Brokerage commissions and taxes have not been considered.

Figure 17.1 shows the 11 years' results of a $10,000 investment in Reuters ADRs from 1986 to 1996. All numbers have been adjusted for stock splits in 1988 and 1994.

FIGURE 17.1   Results of a $10,000 Investment in Reuters Holdings PLC
ADRs in 1986 (Adjusted for Splits)

	Average Share Price	Annual Dividends	Shares Bought from Dividends	Total Shares Owned	Average Value in Year
1986	$10.15	$ 167	16	1,001	$10,162
1987	16.45	280	17	1,018	16,746
1988	13.50	336	25	1,043	14,078
1989	20.45	438	21	1,064	21,767
1990	25.85	617	24	1,088	28,124
1991	23.50	696	29	1,117	26,249
1992	30.90	715	23	1,140	35,226
1993	35.15	752	21	1,161	40,809
1994	43.65	889	20	1,181	51,550
1995	48.65	1,169	24	1,205	58,623
1996	66.00	1,409	21	1,226	80,916

The December 31, 1996, closing price of Reuters Holdings PLC ADRs on the Nasdaq was 76½. At the end of 11 years, your original $10,000 investment had a market value of $93,789, which included reinvested dividends of 7,468. Dividends of $1,409 paid in 1996 represented an effective yield on your original investment of more than 14 percent. The value of the $10,000 investment had multiplied by more than eight times.

Two interesting aspects of an investment in Reuters can be seen in Figure 17.1. First, while the stock price did not pursue a continual upward move (the average price dipped in 1988 and 1991), if you hung on during the down years, you would have benefited in those years because dividends bought more shares at lower prices than at higher prices. Second, your income increased every year, aided by the compounding effect of dividend reinvestment.

Except for 1992, when revenues dipped, Reuters has produced an increasing stream of profits every year for its shareholders. The average PE ratio for Reuters has varied over the 11-year period from as low as 16 times earnings in 1991 to as high as 26 times earnings in 1986. In early 1997 the PE multiple was 19 times earnings.

FIGURE 17.2   Companies for Consideration in an International Stock Portfolio

Company	Where Traded	Ticker Symbol	PE Ratio	Early April 1997 ADR Price	Yield
British Airways	NYSE	BAB	13	104	2.6%
British Petroleum	NYSE	BP	15	131	3.4
British Telecommunications	NYSE	BTY	12	70	5.3
Canon, Inc.	Nasdaq	CANNY	28	112	0.9
Elf Aquitaine	NYSE	ELF	24	47	2.7
ENDESA	NYSE	ELE	11	64	4.4
Telefonica de Espana, S.A.	NYSE	TEF	12	69	2.7
Unilever PLC	NYSE	UL	17	102	4.3

Creating a Portfolio of International Stocks

If you are seeking diversification through global investments, focus on companies whose earnings are growing faster than their industry, their local competitors, and their own historical growth rates. You can search the world for the best growth opportunities. You also need diversification among currencies, economies, and industries. Look for companies that will provide long-term total return (capital appreciation and income). Remember that foreign securities and markets pose different and possibly greater risks than those customarily associated with domestic securities, including currency fluctuations and political instability.

Adding international stocks to an already-diversified mix of U.S. investments can reduce the price volatility of your portfolio. Because the world's markets tend to perform with some degree of independence, a downward trend in U.S. markets may be offset by upward trends in foreign markets. Information on a number of top-quality companies with U.S.-traded ADRs that meet these criteria is shown in Figure 17.2.

What the Companies Do

British Airways.   (202-331-9068). The world's largest airline, British Airways serves 174 destinations in 83 countries. It has a 25 percent interest in Qantas and owns 24.6 percent of USAir. Scheduled passenger service accounts for 92 percent of revenues; 8 percent comes from freight. Since 1987, when the ADRs were listed on the NYSE,

British Airways revenues grew from $5 billion to more than $12 billion in 1996. Earnings increased from $280 million to more than $600 million. The average price of the ADR rose from $30 in 1987 to $87 in 1996.

British Petroleum Company PLC.   (216-586-6220). British Petroleum is one of the largest integrated oil enterprises in the world, with proved reserves of 4.7 billion barrels of oil and 10.4 trillion cubic feet of gas. The company also produces and sells chemicals. Revenues have risen from $40 billion in 1986 to $63 billion in 1996, with profits increasing from about $1 billion to nearly $4 billion. The average price of the ADR rose from $37 in 1986 to $119 in 1996.

British Telecommunications PLC.   (800-331-4568). This company is the principal supplier of telecommunication services in the United Kingdom. It holds an 83 percent market share of business calls and 93 percent of the residential business. Revenues have increased from $15 billion in 1986 to $29 billion in 1996, with profits increasing from $2.4 billion to more than $3 billion. The average price of the ADR rose from $34 in 1986 to $58 in 1996.

Canon, Inc.   (516-488-6700). Canon is a leading Japanese manufacturer of business machines, cameras, and optical products. Copiers account for about 35 percent of sales, with computer peripherals contributing 32 percent and business systems 17 percent. Revenues have increased from $5.5 billion in 1986 to more than $21 billion in 1996, with profits increasing from $66 million to more than $600 million. The average price of the ADR rose from $29 in 1986 to $96 in 1996.

Elf Aquitaine.   (212-922-3004). France's largest corporation and the third largest integrated oil and gas company in Europe, Elf Aquitaine has exploration interests in 26 countries, produces in 15 countries, and has pipeline interests in 5 countries in Europe. Elf Aquitaine also makes chemicals, drugs, and perfumes. It has crude oil reserves of 2.3 billion barrels and natural gas reserves of 6.3 billion cubic feet. Revenues have grown from $18 billion in 1986 to $44 billion in 1996, with profits increasing from $670 million to more than $1.2 billion. The average price of the ADR rose from $10 in 1986 to $39 in 1996.

ENDESA.   (212-750-7200). The largest producer of electricity in Spain, ENDESA accounts for approximately 35 percent of total electric

energy produced in that country. Forty-four percent of its revenue comes from wholesale sources and 47 percent from retail sources, with other sales accounting for the balance. Revenues have grown from $3 billion in 1986 to more than $7 billion in 1996, with profits increasing from $300 million to more than $1 billion. The average price of the ADR rose from $13 in 1988 (when the ADRs began trading) to $61 in 1996.

Telefonica de Espana, S.A.   (011-341-556-8753). This company provides all domestic and international telephone services in Spain and is Spain's largest company. It has 16.1 million phone lines in service (38.7 per 100 inhabitants). The company has 43 percent control of Telefonos de Chile and 8 percent of Telefonica of Argentina. Revenues have grown from $3.4 billion in 1986 to more than $15 billion in 1996, with profits increasing from $800 million to more than $1.3 billion. The average price of the ADR rose from $18 in 1988 to $56 in 1996.

Unilever PLC.   (212-906-3398). Incorporated in Great Britain, Unilever PLC, is a holding company of the Unilever Group. The Unilever Group is one of the world's largest producers and marketers of branded and packaged consumer goods. It operates in 80 countries through 500 operating companies around the world. Principal products include margarine, edible fats and oils, salad dressings, dairy products, frozen foods, ice cream, tea, and many other lines. Revenues have grown from $25 billion in 1986 to more than $50 billion in 1996, with profits increasing from $900 million to more than $2.4 billion. The average price of the ADR rose from $20 in 1988 to $85 in 1996.

Invest the Smart Way

With 60 percent of the world's stock market value represented by companies located abroad, don't overlook this huge investing arena. You can avoid dealing directly with foreign exchanges by purchasing ADRs in U.S. markets. These ADRs entitle you to the same dividends and capital gains accruing to a shareholder who buys shares on an exchange in the home country of the company.

PART THREE

Investing the Smart Way in Bonds

CHAPTER 18

The Basics of Bond Investing

*T*he bond market is huge. The U.S. government is the world's largest borrower, with more than $3 trillion of U.S. Treasury securities outstanding. The mortgage-backed securities market totals more than $4 trillion, the corporate bond market is well over $2 trillion, and there are more than $1.4 trillion of municipal securities in the hands of investors.

A bond is actually an IOU, an acknowledgment by the issuer that money has been borrowed and is to be repaid to the bondholder at a specified rate of interest over a predetermined period. These instruments are referred to as *debt obligations,* contrasted with stocks, which represent ownership of a corporation, usually with the right to vote and receive dividends.

As with most loans, issuers of bonds pay interest for the temporary use of money. The amount borrowed is the principal, or face value, of the bond. The interest you receive is called the bond yield and is expressed as a percentage of the bond's face value. For example, if you pay $1,000 for a bond that pays interest of $80 per year, the bond is said to yield 8 percent ($80 ÷ $1,000). Because your income from the bond generally doesn't vary from year to year, bonds are called *fixed-income securities.*

Fixed-income securities form the centerpiece of most individual investors' portfolios, and with good reason. Bonds have lower but steadier returns than stocks and represent the most reliable source of income. In addition, when added to a portfolio of stocks, bonds act as stabilizers because they reduce the volatility of your overall returns. And while bonds will also reduce the growth potential of your portfolio below that of stocks alone, the real advantage of stock-bond diversification is that it lowers your risk more than it lowers your potential return.

The success of your long-term financial plan depends to a large degree on how you allocate your assets, striking the right balance between bonds, stocks, and cash reserves. (For help in asset allocation, see Chapter 2.)

Avoiding Mistakes through Active Management

Bonds are traded on national exchanges and, like stocks, often sell for more or less than their intrinsic value. This occurs mainly because investors overreact to transitory events in the marketplace or have difficulty understanding today's complex instruments. The best fixed-income investment managers use systematic analytical techniques to identify the best values in the market—bonds yielding more return than appropriate for the risks they entail—and construct optimal bond portfolios.

Many investors mistakenly believe that the best way to invest in bonds is to buy them at issuance and hold them until maturity. But this approach ignores meaningful opportunities to avoid risk and add return. People often focus on yield, believing that higher yields will lead to higher returns. But in reality, yield is a poor indication of total return, which includes capital gains, losses, or both, in addition to interest earned, and determines how the market value of your portfolio has grown. In contrast, managers of many of the best-performing bond mutual funds seek to maximize total returns through active management. They continuously monitor the bond markets in search of sectors, securities, and maturity combinations that hold the greatest return potential.

While the interest paid on issued bonds generally remains fixed, general interest rates, credit ratings, yield curves, and market conditions are constantly changing. Buying a portfolio of bonds and putting them aside with the intention of holding them until maturity means you'll miss attractive investment opportunities as they come along and leave yourself vulnerable to new and unanticipated risks. And even if you're willing to forgo opportunity and take on risk for the sake of predictable interest income, you can't be sure about your own future needs. With a buy-and-hold strategy, you may end up locking yourself into a bond that you will later need to liquidate at a low point in its market value. Generally, active management of a bond portfolio is far more profitable and prudent than buy-and-hold investing.

Managing Risk in Bond Portfolios

Many top managers of fixed-income investment portfolios like to maintain the duration, or interest-rate sensitivity, of their portfolios at levels close to those of short-term bonds (those with maturities of one to five years) and intermediate-term bonds (those with maturities of five to ten years). Duration is a risk-measuring gauge that provides a means of measuring in advance how much a bond or bond investment will rise or fall in value when interest rates change. It takes into account not only the maturity of an interest-bearing investment, but also the present and future flow of interest payments. This produces a figure, stated in years, that can be multiplied by a percentage-point change in interest rates to get the percentage change you can expect in the price of an investment. The rule of thumb is, the longer the maturity, the greater the price change in response to interest-rate changes.

Shorter duration gives portfolios the risk-reward characteristics of short- and intermediate-term bonds. Short-term bonds generally outperform money-market investments with little more volatility, while intermediates are much safer than long-term bonds yet offer about the same income and return.

The investor who is searching for the right combination of yield and safety faces many investment choices. Banks offer federally insured money-market accounts and certificates of deposits. But bank rates generally have not been competitive in recent years as the banking industry works to boost its profitability.

The yield can pick up substantially when moving from bank deposits to a variety of short- and long-term debt instruments. Money-market funds offer rates and an expectation of principal stability, though without the protection of federal deposit insurance. And, because interest rates on long-term instruments are significantly higher today, the yield of longer-term bonds can be well above that of money-market funds. The risk of progressively larger fluctuations in principal value is the trade-off an investor must accept for higher yields and more durable income. Listed in Figure 18.1 are the average yields of various categories of debt instruments in early 1997.

FIGURE 18.1 Yields of Debt Instruments

Categories	Average Yields
Tax-Free Money-Market Funds	2.87%
U.S. Treasury Notes (10-Year) Inflation*	3.47
Taxable Money-Market Funds	4.93
U.S. Treasury Bills (13-Week)	5.03
Tax-free Municipal Bonds	5.80
U.S. Treasury Notes (10-Year)	6.57
U.S. Treasury Bonds (30-Year)	6.85
High-Grade Corporate Bonds	7.18
Intermediate-Grade Corporate Bonds	7.38
Low-Grade Corporate Bonds (Junk Bonds)	9.51

*Principal amount is realized at maturity and rises with inflation.

Here, the age-old warning of "caveat emptor" applies. Selecting investments on the basis of yield alone can be dangerous to your wealth. Higher yield is usually associated with higher risks. Higher risks generally arise from lower credit quality or longer maturities. Lower credit quality involves the risk of default, that is, the failure of an issuer to make principal or interest payments when due.

How the Yield Curve Works

After you have decided on your investment objectives, and what kind of an investor you are, your challenge is to find a comfortable balance between risk and reward. In the world of fixed-income investments, a useful tool in attaining that balance is the *yield curve,* a graph that correlates bond yields to maturities. The yield curve plots the yields of bonds of the same credit quality against their maturity periods, from one month to 30 years. The degree of difference between yields of the shortest and longest maturities, which also can be seen as the premium that investors can expect in return for a long-term commitment, defines the slope of the curve. Using the curve's rate structure as a reference, you can assemble a bond portfolio that correlates with your investment objectives and tolerance for risk. For example, Figure 18.2 illustrates the Treasury yield curve on March 11, 1997, showing the yield percentage of selected Treasury securities.

FIGURE 18.2   Treasury Yield Curve

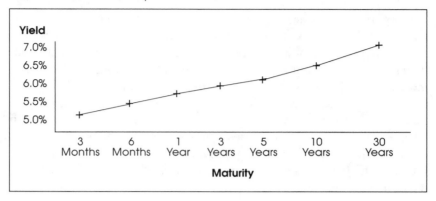

As a bond buyer, you need to be aware of the fundamental relationship between a bond's yield (its interest income) and its maturity. Longer maturities generally, but not always, translate into higher coupon rates (a bond's stated interest rate) because of the increased potential that, over time, a rise in interest rates will lower bond prices.

Generally, bond values move in the opposite direction from interest rates. Thus, if interest rates go up, the price of bonds will decline. Conversely, when interest rates go down, the value of bonds will rise. For example, suppose you own a $1,000 face amount bond that pays 8 percent ($80 per year) and want to sell it. But you find that similar bonds of the same quality and maturity are now paying 9 percent. To sell, your bond would have to be priced at an amount that would provide a prospective buyer with a 9 percent yield. Thus, you would be able to sell it for approximately $889, because the annual interest of $80 on a bond with a cost of $889 provides a yield of 9 percent ($80 divided by $889).

Types of Bonds at a Glance

Bond issuers fall into three categories:

1. Corporations
2. The U.S. government and its agencies
3. States, municipalities, and other local governments

Each has features and disadvantages you should be aware of when deciding which type of bond best meets your investment needs.

Corporate Bonds

Corporate bonds are issued by corporations to finance their long-term capital projects and are paid back within a specified length of time (called the bond's maturity). To help you in making a judgment about the creditworthiness of a bond, you can check its evaluation by one or more independent rating services. Rating services take a number of factors into consideration, including the issuing company's ability to repay the face value of the bond. We'll look closely at bond ratings in Chapter 19. In general, the interest rate paid reflects the bond's relative safety. Usually, the higher the quality, the lower the interest rate. The interest rate also reflects the bond's maturity; the longer the maturity, the higher the interest paid.

U.S. Government Bonds

U.S. government bonds can take the form of Treasury securities or securities of certain U.S. agencies, such as those of the Government National Mortgage Association (GNMA), called "Ginnie Maes." These instruments are backed by the full faith and credit of the U.S. government as to the timely payment of principal and interest. Other U.S. agency securities, such as those of the Federal National Mortgage Association, called "Fannie Maes," carry a less formal indirect backing.

Depending on their length of maturity, Treasury issues are designated as U.S. Treasury bills (with maturities from 90 days to one year), U.S. Treasury notes (maturing in one to ten years), and U.S. Treasury bonds (carrying 10- to 30-year maturities).

State and Local Government Bonds

Municipal bonds are issued by state and local governments, often to finance specific projects such as highways, schools, recreational facilities, and so on. While they typically pay lower rates than corporate bonds, the interest income is generally exempt from federal income taxes and frequently from state and local taxes, as well. Thus, a lower yield bond actually can be more attractive than a higher paying taxable security when you figure what the relative tax consequences would be, especially in the higher tax brackets.

Even though less than 1 percent of municipal bonds default, a few well-publicized defaults have resulted in great demand for insured bonds. Demand for insurance is so great that about 40 percent of new local government issues are insured. (For an in-depth discussion of municipal bonds, see Chapter 21.)

How Returns Are Calculated

The total return of a bond is the change in value of your investment over a particular period, assuming that all interest payments have been reinvested. Two components added together determine a bond's total return:

1. *Yield (interest income).* When you purchase a bond for $1,000 paying $80 interest, for instance, you can expect to receive an annualized yield of 8 percent, the bond's interest income reflected as a percentage of the purchase price.
2. *Capital return.* Yield or interest income is not the only way of determining how profitable your investment has been. While the issuer of a bond promises to pay its face value at maturity, the value of your bond may fluctuate between the issue date and maturity date, usually because of an upward or downward movement in interest rates. Thus, a $1,000 bond coming due in the year 2008 may today be worth $900 or $1,000, depending on whether interest rates in general are higher or lower than the rate paid by your bond. This rise or fall in the value of your principal is known as *capital return.*

If a $1,000 bond drops in price to $950, your capital return would be –5 percent. Add that to the bond's 8 percent yield and your total return becomes approximately 3 percent [8% yield + (–5% capital return)]. On the other hand, if your bond rises in price to $1,050, the total return on your bond increases to approximately 13 percent (8% yield + 5% capital return).

Factors Affecting Total Return

Interest rates. The first factor that can affect the total return you receive on your fixed-income investment is a change that may take place in interest rates. As noted earlier, generally the market value of bonds moves in the opposite direction from interest rates. So, the value of your bonds declines if interest rates go up, and it rises if interest rates go down. As discussed earlier, market risk is the degree to which a bond's price fluctuates as a result of changes in interest rates.

FIGURE 18.3   Effect of Interest Rate Changes on Bond Prices

| Bond Maturity | Initial Principal of $1,000 and Yield of 10% | | | |
	1% Rise in Rates		1% Decline in Rates	
Short-term (2.5-year maturity)	$979	−2.1%	$1,022	+2.2%
Intermediate-term (7-year maturity)	952	−4.8	1,051	+5.1
Long-term (20-year maturity)	920	−8.0	1,092	+9.2

Maturity.   A bond's maturity also affects how much its value is apt to rise of fall. Bonds with longer maturities usually offer higher yields, but also tend to have more volatile price swings than those with shorter maturities. The longer the life of a bond (its maturity), the greater the degree of price fluctuation. Consequently, more cautious investors typically prefer shorter-term bonds because their exposure to volatility is much less.

Figure 18.3 shows how the prices of bonds with varying maturities would respond following a 1 percent change in interest rates. As you can see, rising interest rates result in decreasing bond values and vice versa. Further, the degree of volatility increases as maturities lengthen. Note how much more volatility affects the values of long-term bonds than those of intermediate- or short-term bonds.

Credit quality.   While interest rates and maturity can influence the face value of a bond, a bond's credit quality has an important bearing on its yield. Credit risk is the chance that your bond will default (fail to make timely payment of principal and interest). Lower-quality bonds usually offer higher yields but also have a greater risk of default.

Independent rating services evaluate many factors to determine a bond's credit quality, including the issuing company or agency's ability to repay the face value of the bond. Standard & Poor's Corporation and Moody's Investors Service are the two best-known ratings services that regularly evaluate issuers. They issue ratings that range from the highest quality rating (Aaa for U.S. Treasury securities) to the so-called "junk bonds" of corporations whose financial health may be considered weak.

Just as interest rates and bond values have an inverse relationship, the creditworthiness of an issuer and the interest paid have a similar relationship. For instance, the safest investment you can make, guaranteed by the full faith and credit of the U.S. government as to the timely payment of principal and interest, usually pays a lower interest rate. As you move down the scale to less creditworthy and, therefore, more speculative bonds, the issuer is forced to pay a higher interest rate to compensate for the greater risk.

Invest the Smart Way

*B*onds generally produce a higher and steadier flow of income than you would receive from money-market funds or bank savings accounts, and the amount invested is usually at less risk than if you had invested it in stocks. Before investing in bonds, though, assess the bonds' market and credit risk to determine whether they are compatible with your personal risk tolerance level.

CHAPTER 19

How Bonds Are Rated for Safety

*I*f you're safety conscious, it generally doesn't pay to invest in lower-quality bonds—stick with high-quality investments. For the utmost credit safety, choose U.S. Treasury obligations. The next safest are U.S. government agency obligations. There are also many top-quality corporate and municipal bonds that are "investment-grade" and considered very safe. Avoid money-market funds investing in below–top-tier instruments and bonds that are below investment-grade (junk bonds) unless you understand and are willing to accept the risks.

Most corporate and many municipal bonds carry a letter-coded rating to indicate their relative quality. Mutual funds that include corporate or municipal bonds and other debt instruments in their portfolios specify the credit quality of bonds in which they are permitted to invest. Rating systems have been developed by several widely recognized investment services, and many bonds, but not all, are evaluated by these services to determine the probability of default by the issuers.

Moody's Investors Service, Inc., Standard & Poor's Corporation, Duff & Phelps, and Fitch's Investors Service are the major firms that analyze the financial strength of each bond's issuer, whether a corporation or a government body. Bonds are assigned ratings by these firms to assist in determining the suitability of a particular instrument for investment purposes. For example, Standard & Poor's classifies investment-grade bonds as AAA, AA, A, and BBB. Anything lower is speculative; institutions that invest other people's money may not, under most state laws, buy them.

Because an issuer must pay a substantial amount to obtain a rating by one of these services, debt securities are often issued on an unrated basis. This is particularly true if the total value of the offering is deemed insufficient to justify the cost of obtaining a rating. So, the fact that a bond issue is unrated does not by itself necessarily indicate that it is an unsound investment.

Corporate Bonds

Following is a brief description of the corporate bond rating system used by Moody's Investors Service (used with permission), which is somewhat similar to Standard & Poor's:

- *Aaa.* Bonds rated Aaa are judged to be of the best quality. They carry the smallest degree of investment risk and are generally referred to as "gilt-edge." Interest payments are protected by a large or exceptionally stable margin and principal is secure. Though the various protective elements are likely to change, potential changes are most unlikely to impair the fundamentally strong position of such issues.
- *Aa.* Bonds rated Aa are judged to be of high quality by all standards. Together with the Aaa group, they constitute what are generally known as high-grade bonds. They are rated lower than the best bonds because margins of protection may not be as large as those for Aaa securities; there may be greater fluctuation of protective elements, or other elements may be present that make the long-term risks appear somewhat larger than those in Aaa securities.
- *A.* Bonds rated A possess many favorable investment attributes and are considered upper-medium-grade obligations. Factors giving security to principal and interest are considered adequate, but elements may be present that suggest a susceptibility to impairment sometime in the future.
- *Baa.* Bonds rated Baa are considered medium-grade obligations, that is, they are neither highly protected nor poorly secured. Interest payments and principal security appear adequate for the present, but certain protective elements may be lacking or may be characteristically unreliable over any great length of time. Such bonds lack outstanding investment characteristics and, in fact, have speculative characteristics as well.

- *Ba.* Bonds rated Ba are judged to have speculative elements. Their future cannot be considered assured. Often the protection of interest and principal payments may be moderate and, therefore, not sufficiently secure during both good and bad times over the future. Uncertainty of position characterizes bonds in this class.
- *B.* Bonds rated B generally lack characteristics of the desirable investment. Assurance of interest and principal payments or maintenance of other terms of the contract over any long period of time may be small.
- *Caa.* Bonds rated Caa are of poor standing. Such issues may be in default, or elements of danger may exist with respect to principal or interest.
- *Ca.* Bonds rated Ca represent obligations that are highly speculative. Such issues are often in default or have other marked shortcomings.
- *C.* Bonds rated C are the lowest-rated class of bonds, and issues can be regarded as having extremely poor prospects of ever attaining any real investment standing.

Moody's applies the numerical modifiers 1, 2, and 3 in each generic rating classification from Aa through B in its corporate bond rating system. The modifier 1 indicates that the security ranks in the higher end of its generic rating category, 2 indicates a midrange ranking, and 3 indicates that the issue ranks in the lower end.

Municipal Bonds

As is the case with debt securities issued by corporations, credit risk should be considered in connection with bonds issued by states and municipalities. An investor who buys individual tax-free securities or tax-free mutual fund shares should be concerned about the possibility that a bond issuer will fail to make timely payments of interest or principal to a portfolio. The credit risk of a portfolio depends on the credit quality of its underlying securities. In general, the lower the credit quality of a portfolio's municipal securities, the higher a portfolio's yield, all other factors (such as maturity) being equal.

Below is a brief description of the municipal bond rating system used by Moody's Investors Service (used with permission).

Definitions of Long-Term Ratings

- *Aaa.* Bonds rated Aaa are judged to be the best quality. They carry the smallest degree of investment risk and are generally referred to as "gilt-edged."
- *Aa.* Bonds rated Aa are judged to be of high quality by all standards. Together with the Aaa group, they comprise what are generally known as high-grade bonds.
- *A.* Bonds rated A possess many favorable investment attributes and are considered as upper-medium-grade obligations.
- *Baa.* Bonds rated Baa are considered medium-grade issues, that is, they are neither highly protected nor poorly secured.
- *Ba.* Bonds rated Ba are judged to have speculative elements. Future payment of interest and principal cannot be considered as well assured.
- *B.* Bonds rated B generally lack characteristics of the desirable investment. Assurance of interest and principal payments or maintenance of other terms of the contract over any long period of time may be small.
- *Caa.* Bonds rated Caa are of poor standing. Such issues may be in default or there may be present elements of danger with respect to principal or interest.
- *Ca.* Bonds rated Ca represent obligations that are speculative to a high degree. Such issues are often in default or have other marked shortcomings.
- *C.* Bonds rated C are the lowest rated class of bonds, and issues so rated can be regarded as having extremely poor prospects of ever attaining any real investment standing.
- *NR.* Not rated.

Definitions of Short-Term Loan Ratings

- MIG ratings terminate at the retirement of the obligation, while a VMIG rating expiration will be a function of each issue's specific structural or credit features.
- *MIG 1/VMIG 1.* This designation denotes best quality. There is a strong protection by established cash flows, superior liquidity support, or demonstrated broad-based access to the market for refinancing.

- *MIG 2/VMIG 2.* This designation denotes high quality. Margins of protection are ample, although not so large as in the preceding group.
- *MIG 3/VMIG 3.* This designation denotes favorable quality. Liquidity and cash-flow protection may be narrow, and market access for refinancing is likely to be less well established.
- *SG.* This designation denotes speculative quality. Debt insurance in this category may lack margins of protection.

Invest the Smart Way

*T*o reduce credit risk when buying bonds, include only investment-grade (BBB or better) bonds in your portfolio; lower-rated debt securities are considered speculative. If you're safety conscious and want the utmost credit safety, choose U.S. Treasury obligations.

CHAPTER 20

Profiting from U.S. Treasury Securities

*T*oday, interest in U.S. Treasury securities has increased because of their high quality and yield compared with other debt securities.

You can buy treasuries with a wide range of maturities to help you satisfy a variety of investment objectives. They are considered among the safest of all investments because payment of interest and principal is guaranteed by the full faith and credit of the U.S. government. Treasuries offer predictable income, which is generally exempt from state and local taxes and repayment of principal in full if held to maturity.

Ample liquidity is available through an active secondary market. The secondary market for treasuries is the largest such market for any type of security. Through a broker, you have the opportunity to sell your investment prior to maturity or purchase issued securities. As is true with stock and bond investments, your purchases or sales will be subject to prevailing market prices. Prices of many treasury securities will increase as interest rates fall and decrease as rates rise, so you may have a gain or loss if you sell prior to maturity.

How Treasuries Can Help Your Investment Portfolio

Diversification is important in any portfolio. By spreading your investments over different classes of assets, rather than having all your eggs in one basket, you take advantage of a proven investment principle that moderates risk. Most investors with diversified portfolios have a portion of their holdings in bonds and short-term securities. As one of the safest investments available, treasuries are an attractive investment option. Consider the advantages they offer:

- *Safety.* Treasuries are considered the safest fixed-income investments, because they are guaranteed by the full faith and credit of the U.S. government for the prompt payment of interest, and, if you hold your treasury securities to maturity, you will receive the full face value regardless of market conditions. Your income from Treasury securities is fully predictable for as long as you hold them.
- *Flexibility.* Treasuries can be ideal investments for either the short or the long term. With the wide range of maturities available and an active secondary market (for ready liquidity), structuring a portfolio is easy and will help you meet investment goals, such as saving for a down payment on a home, college tuition, or retirement income.
- *Income.* With treasuries, a steady stream of interest income will help you meet both short- and long-term needs. The income can be used to supplement retirement income, provide for current expenses, or build an emergency fund. Or, it can be reinvested for capital appreciation through interest compounding.
- *Tax advantages.* Although the interest on your treasury securities is subject to federal taxes, it is exempt from state and local taxes. If you live in a state with high income taxes, you may actually keep more of what interest you earn than you would with comparable taxable investments.

Treasury Securities You Can Buy

Short-term T-bills have 3-, 6-, or 12-month maturities, and are sold at a discount from face value. The difference between the price you pay and the face value you receive at maturity represents your interest earned. *Treasury notes* (T-notes), with 2-, 3-, 5-, or 10-year maturities, and *Treasury bonds* (T-bonds), with 30-year maturity, are medium- to long-term investments that pay interest semiannually. The interest rate you earn on T-notes and T-bonds is locked in at the time of purchase and is not affected by changing market conditions. The rate remains the

FIGURE 20.1 A Summary of U.S. Treasury Securities

Issue	Maturities	Auction Schedule	Minimum Face Value*
T-Bills	3 and 6 months	Weekly	$10,000
	1 year	Monthly	10,000
T-Notes	2 years	Monthly	5,000
	3 years	Quarterly: February, May, August, November	5,000
	5 years	Monthly	1,000
	10 years	Quarterly: February, May, August, November	1,000
T-Bonds	30 years	Semiannually: February, August	1,000
Zeros	6 months to 30 years	Available in secondary market only	5,000

*Thereafter, you can buy in $1,000 increments. Face value is the amount you will receive if the security is held to maturity.

same until you sell your security or it matures. *Zero-coupon treasuries* (zeros), also called STRIPS (separate trading of registered interest and principal of securities), the Treasury's acronym for its own zero-coupon securities, are sold at deep discounts. Zeros pay no interest during their life; interest is reinvested over the life of the security at the stated rate and paid only at maturity. Even though the interest from zeros isn't available to you until the bonds mature, the interest they earn each year is subject to federal income taxes.

Figure 20.1 provides a summary of treasury securities. Except for zeros, you can buy U.S. Treasury securities at periodic auctions directly from the Federal Reserve (see Chapter 25) or through a broker in the secondary market. Zeros are available in the secondary market only.

A new kind of treasury security was introduced to the public in 1996: the *inflation-indexed* security. Inflation-indexed securities give individual and institutional investors a chance to buy a security that keeps pace with inflation. When you buy inflation-indexed securities, the Treasury pays you interest on the inflation-adjusted principal amount. Competitive bidding before the security's issue determines the fixed-interest or coupon rate. Semiannual interest payments are deter-

FIGURE 20.2   Bond Laddering

Maturity	Interest Rate	Invested Amount
1 year	6.00%	$10,000
2 years	6.25	10,000
3 years	6.50	10,000
4 years	6.75	10,000
5 years	7.00	10,000

mined by multiplying the inflation-adjusted principal amount by one-half the stated rate of interest on each interest payment date. At maturity, your securities are redeemed at their inflation-adjusted principal or the original par amount, whichever is greater. Inflation-indexed securities are available in multiples of $1,000. The minimum is $1,000.

The Bond Laddering Strategy

To diversify holdings, moderate interest-rate risk, and preserve capital, many investors tailor an investment strategy called *bond laddering*. The idea behind this strategy is to invest in treasuries with different maturities so that funds become available for reinvestment periodically. This same technique may be used when investing in corporate and municipal bonds.

The chart shown in Figure 20.2 gives an example of bond laddering. It shows a five-year ladder made up of different Treasury issues. In this example, you are investing $50,000 in Treasury securities of varying maturities. This laddered portfolio provides a "blended" (or average) yield of 6.5 percent. Your objectives are achieved by spreading the maturities over evenly spaced future dates.

Bond laddering offers you several advantages:

- Laddering makes it easy to diversify the maturities of your bond holdings, lessening the effects of uncertainty in a changeable interest-rate environment.
- During a time of low rates, laddering provides a way to avoid having an entire fixed-income portfolio locked into a set yield for years to come.

- If rates rise, you can reinvest your maturing bonds at higher rates. If rates fall, you have the protection afforded by the portion of your portfolio that is invested at higher rates.
- Laddering gives the certainty of having available the principal you need on future dates to meet specific goals. By scheduling maturity dates, you can have the assurance that the funds you're counting on will be available when needed.

U.S. Savings Bonds

Like other treasury securities, savings bonds are backed by the full faith and credit of the U.S. government, and the interest they pay is exempt from state and local taxes. However, savings bonds have several features that make them quite different from other treasuries.

Savings bonds can be purchased at any bank, or through your company by payroll deduction, in denominations ranging from as little as $50 to as much as $10,000. The government limits you to investing a maximum of $15,000 in any one year in savings bonds.

Series EE savings bonds pay no coupon interest. Instead, they sell for one-half their face value and are redeemed at full face value upon maturity. In these "accrual-type" bonds, interest is paid when the bond is cashed in, before or on maturity and not regularly over the life of the bond. Thus, a $50 bond costs $25 and a $10,000 bond costs $5,000. Federal tax on the accrued interest you have earned is not payable until you redeem the bond.

The interest rate on Series EE bonds purchased on or after May 1, 1995, is market-based. Bonds held more than five years earn interest equal to 85 percent of the average yield that five-year Treasury securities earned during the period the bond was held. Investors who hold bonds less than five years get a market-based rate equal to 85 percent of the average yield that six-month T-bills earned during the bonds' life. No interest is credited on bonds that are held less than six months.

Interest on savings bonds is credited every six months from the month of purchase. It is important, therefore, that you redeem your EE bonds right after their six-month anniversary. If you redeem prior to that date, you may lose up to several months' interest. And here's a money-making tip: Because interest begins to accrue on the first day of the month of purchase, it makes good sense to buy bonds at the end of the month.

For really long-term investors, there is a safety net to protect them against very low interest rates. If a savings bond has not reached face value after 17 years, the Treasury can raise it to that level in a one-time adjustment.

Series HH bonds are a current income security available at par (purchase price equals face value) in denominations of $500, $1,000, $5,000, and $10,000. HH bonds are not available for cash purchase but may be obtained in exchange for Series E bonds and Series EE bonds. They also may be obtained through the authorized reinvestment of matured Series H bonds. A minimum of $500 in redemption value of older bonds is necessary in order to make an exchange. Series HH bonds pay interest semiannually at a fixed rate that prevails at the time of exchange (currently 4 percent). That rate is set for the first ten years that the bond is held and can change when the bond enters an extension period for another ten years. Interest payments are transmitted by direct deposit to the owner's designated account at a financial institution. You get the interest twice a year and receive your original purchase price at redemption.

For a good, free guide, write for *The Savings Bonds Question and Answer Book,* Office of Public Affairs, U.S. Savings Bonds Division, Department of the Treasury, Washington, DC, 20226. Current interest rate information on U.S. savings bonds can be obtained by calling toll-free 800-487-2663.

Invest the Smart Way

U.S. Treasury bonds, among the safest of all investments, are available with a wide range of maturities and can be structured to achieve a variety of investment objectives. With them you can achieve predictable income, exemption from state and local taxes, and repayment of principal in full if held to maturity.

CHAPTER 21

Reducing Your Taxes with Municipal Bonds

*M*ost investors carefully evaluate yield, safety, and growth potential when they choose an investment. Yet, few stop to consider the effect of taxes on their investment return. For instance, an investor in the 36 percent tax bracket could be giving up $36 of every $100 of investment income to taxes. From a different perspective, if this investor has an 8 percent income return, it equals just 5.12 percent after taxes.

Municipal bonds, often called "munis," appeal to investors for two reasons:

1. *Tax-free income.* Municipal bonds are one of the few remaining sources of tax-free income. They provide income that is exempt from Federal income taxes, and, in the state of issue, municipal bonds are often free from state and local taxes as well. For instance, the state of New York might issue a bond to help pay for repaving a tollway, then use the money collected from the tolls to repay investors. The interest income from this bond would be exempt from federal income taxes, and for New York residents the interest would also be exempt from state and city taxes.

   Income from some municipal bonds is subject to the federal alternative minimum tax (AMT), which applies to certain high-income investors. Such investors should check to see if a bond they are considering is subject to AMT before investing.

2. *Diversification.* Bonds have investment characteristics quite different from those of common stocks. Though bond prices are sometimes quite volatile, they are generally considered safer than stocks and can serve to diversify an equity-heavy portfolio. Municipal bonds are generally considered to be high on the investment safety scale, second only to securities issued by the U.S. government and its agencies.

Tax-free investments have been gaining in popularity. According to Bond Buyer magazine, over 75 percent of municipal obligations are owned by individual investors through investments in individual bonds and mutual funds. With more than $1.25 trillion of municipal debt outstanding, the sheer size of the tax-free bond market helps to make it stable and liquid, so buying and selling bonds is relatively easy.

What Are Municipal Bonds?

Municipal bonds are interest-bearing securities issued by state and local governments to support their financial needs or to finance public projects. A municipal bond obligates the issuer to pay the bondholder a fixed amount of interest periodically and to repay the principal value of the bond on a specified maturity date. Like bonds issued by corporations or the U.S. government, municipal bonds are considered fixed-income securities, because they offer a steady rate of interest income. They are often called *debt obligations,* as they represent a loan to the bond issuer.

Types of Municipal Bonds

General obligation (GO) bonds. GO bonds are issued by municipal agencies, such as cities or states, that have taxing authority. Payments of principal and interest on GO bonds are secured by the full faith and credit of the issuer. Thus, the issuing agency promises to use every means available to ensure prompt payment of principal and interest, when due.

Revenue bonds. Revenue bonds are payable from a specific source of income. Sources of income frequently used to pay revenue bond issues include tolls and rents or charges from facilities such as turnpikes, airports, hospitals, and water treatment plants.

FIGURE 21.1 Tax-Free versus Taxable Income

Taxable Income		Federal Tax Rate	Assumed Tax-Free Yields				
Single Return	Joint Return		4.00%	5.00%	6.00%	7.00%	8.00%
			Equivalent Taxable Yield				
To 24,000	To $40,100	15 %	4.71%	5.88%	7.06%	8.24%	9.41%
$24,001–58,150	$40,101–96,900	28	5.56	6.94	8.33	9.72	11.11
$58,151–121,300	$96,901–147,700	31	5.80	7.25	8.70	10.14	11.59
$121,301–263,750	147,701–263,750	36	6.25	7.81	9.38	10.94	12.50
Over $263,750	Over $263,750	39.6	6.62	8.28	9.93	11.59	13.25

The equivalent taxable yields are calculated based on the maximum marginal tax rate at each tax bracket in effect in 1996. These brackets are subject to change. See your tax adviser regarding more recent tax legislation and how tax laws affect your own personal financial situation.

The Rewards of Tax-Free Investing

Because the interest from municipal bonds is exempt from federal tax, these securities generally pay lower interest rates than similar taxable investments. Nevertheless, because the interest income is exempt from federal and, in some cases, state and local income taxes, you may actually keep more spendable income from the tax-free security.

Figure 21.1 illustrates the effect of tax-free versus taxable income at different income levels and tax rates. To compare how the two investments might work for you, locate your annual income, after deductions and exemptions, and then read across to find the yield you would need on a taxable investment to match the tax-free yield at various rates. For example, a person in the 31 percent tax bracket must earn 10.14 percent from a fully taxable investment to equal a 7 percent yield that is exempt from federal income tax. With state and local taxes taken into consideration, the difference could be even more dramatic.

Municipal Bond Investment Risks

As is true with corporate bonds, interest rate risk and credit risk are two major factors you should assess before investing in a municipal bond.

Insured Municipal Bonds

When Orange County, California, filed for bankruptcy in late 1994, it sent shock waves through the investment community. Orange County was the biggest U.S. municipality ever to take that action. One way municipal bond investors can protect themselves from the risk of default is by purchasing triple-A rated insured municipal bonds. The higher credit quality, of course, means you will earn a slightly lower yield. Holders of insured bonds are guaranteed they will continue to receive principal and interest payments on time and in full if their bonds default. Although uninsured Orange County bonds were downgraded after its financial problems became known, its triple-A insured bonds were not.

Even though less than 1 percent of local government bonds default, demand for insurance is great enough that about 40 percent of new local government issues are insured, giving them a triple-A rating. Aside from the protection against default, many investors choose insured bonds because the extra protection and triple-A rating insulates them from the uncertainty that sometimes depresses prices and makes it difficult to sell bonds that are involved in controversy even though they have not defaulted.

Major insurers of municipal bonds—all members of the Association of Financial Guaranty Insurors (AFGI)—include AMBAC Indemnity Corporation, Capital Guaranty Insurance Company, Financial Guaranty Insurance Company, Financial Security Assurance, Inc., and Municipal Bond Investors Assurance Corporation. Each of these companies' claims-paying ability is rated triple-A by one or more of the major rating agencies. In the 25 years of the bond insurance industry, no investor in a bond insured by an AFGI member company has ever failed to receive a bond payment, and no AFGI-insured bond has ever been downgraded from triple-A.

Invest the Smart Way

*M*unicipal bonds can provide you with one of the few remaining sources of tax-free income. The interest they pay is exempt from federal income taxes and in some cases is exempt from state and local taxes. Furthermore, although sometimes volatile in price, municipal bonds are generally considered more conservative than stocks and can serve to balance an equity-laden portfolio.

CHAPTER 22

Getting Your Corporate Bond's Worth

If you are seeking investments with a higher rate of return compared to other fixed-income securities, you may want to consider corporate bonds. You have a wide variety of issues to choose from, including utilities, transportation companies, and industrial corporations.

Corporate bonds are debt instruments issued by corporations to raise capital for expansion and other corporate purposes. You, as an investor, lend money to the corporation. The corporation (the issuer) in turn promises to pay you the principal amount at a preset date. The issuer also promises to make interest payments to you on a periodic basis, usually every six months. This interest generally is at a fixed rate set when the bond is issued, although some bonds are issued where the interest rate may float in relation to the prevailing interest rates until the bond matures.

The corporate bond market is well over $2 trillion, with an active secondary market where securities may be bought and sold through brokers subsequent to original issuance. However, some types of bonds are less actively traded than others, so an investor may have less liquidity.

Corporate Bond Yields

Corporate bonds generally offer higher yields than government Treasury bonds and municipal securities. However, they also carry more risk. Maturities of corporate instruments range from a few weeks to more than 30 years. Interest is typically paid semiannually. Some corporate bonds are offered as zero-coupon issues, selling at a deep discount from face value. The face value, which represents both principal and accrued interest, is paid at maturity.

Credit Risk

Even though payments to bond investors take precedence over dividend payments to stockholders of a corporation, you, the potential investor, should consider the safety of the issue. The quality of a corporate bond is based on an evaluation of the issuer's financial ability to pay interest and return your principal. Corporate bonds generally have no government backing. If a company files for bankruptcy, your investment may be in jeopardy.

To help determine a bond's creditworthiness, many investors rely on one or two major rating agencies, Moody's Investors Service or Standard & Poor's Corporation, to grade issues in terms of safety. Higher-rated bonds tend to be safer and usually offer a lower yield. Bonds offering higher yields generally have lower credit ratings.

Always check the quality rating of a potential bond investment before you purchase it. And, because the financial health of a company can change, monitoring a corporate bond's rating periodically is important. A change in the quality rating of a bond can affect its liquidity and value. (For more information on this topic, see Chapter 19.)

Interest Rate Risk

The current yield of a bond moves up or down in response to changes in prevailing interest rates. If interest rates go up, the price of an outstanding bond will go down because any new bond would be issued at the prevailing higher rates. If interest rates go down, the price will go up. Therefore, if your sell a bond early, the price will be subject to the current interest rate environment. (For an explanation of how this works, see Chapter 18.) If you hold a bond to maturity, of course, you should receive the face value.

Types of Corporate Bonds

Although all corporate bonds are similar in purpose, each falls into one of the following five major classifications:

1. *Debenture bonds* are backed by the overall financial health of the company issuing the bond. Because there is no collateral, these bonds represent a greater level of risk and generally offer a higher rate of return.
2. *Collateralized bonds* are backed by assets that the issuer puts up as collateral for the bonds. For instance, capital assets backing a bond may include real estate holdings and equipment.
3. *Callable bonds* can be redeemed by the issuer prior to maturity at a predetermined price. They often will offer higher yields than noncallable bonds.
4. *"Sinking fund" bonds* require the issuer to deposit money in a sinking fund with the bond trustee. The sinking fund money is used either to redeem the bond at par prior to maturity or to repay the principal at maturity.
5. *Convertible bonds* can be exchanged by the investor for common stock in the issuing company. This investment offers you the potential for capital appreciation from the underlying common stock. Because convertibles generally sell at a premium to the conversion value of the stock, however, these bonds usually offer lower yields than comparable quality nonconvertibles. (For a full description of this investment opportunity, see Chapter 23.)

Owning Bonds versus Bond Mutual Funds

Does it make more sense for you to buy bonds or to buy bond mutual funds? There are advantages and disadvantages of each approach.

There are three basic reasons for owning individual bonds:

1. You can ensure that you will not lose money. Do this by buying top-quality bonds like treasuries or AAA municipals that will mature when you need the funds. Holding the bonds until maturity guarantees your principal back. By contrast, most mutual funds don't offer you a maturity date. You may or may not get your money back, depending on the fund's market value at the time you sell.

2. You pay the same price as the big institutions, avoiding sales charges, if you buy new bonds. The issuer absorbs the commission. At maturity, or when the bond is called, you can redeem it through the issuer's paying agent, at no charge.
3. If you invest in treasury securities or other AAA-rated bonds, you don't need to worry about diversification to reduce risk from default.

There are five basic reasons for owning bond mutual funds:

1. You can invest small amounts. Your initial purchase can be as little as $500, and additional investments can be for as little as $50.
2. Dividends can be reinvested automatically. This is important if you don't need the income to live on. Imagine the difficulty in trying to reinvest a $300 semiannual interest payment you receive from an individual bond investment. You are pretty much limited to a money-market fund or bank interest.
3. You can minimize costs by buying no-load bond funds from companies with low expenses. This allows you to buy without a commission and realize higher yields.
4. Mutual funds are a good idea if you aren't sure when you'll need your money. Fund shares can be redeemed at a better price than you'd get for individual bonds sold before maturity. Small dollar amounts of bonds fetch lower prices in the market than institutions get when they sell in large amounts.
5. With even a minimum bond fund investment, you get the same diversification as an investor putting in millions of dollars. This is especially important if you are interested in lower-quality bonds in order to achieve a higher yield. Some of those bonds will probably default. To minimize risk, you need to own a piece of many different issues.

Invest the Smart Way

Corporate bonds continue to be important investment choices for investors seeking a higher rate of return compared to other fixed-income securities. Corporate bonds generally offer higher yields than municipal and Treasury bonds, but they also carry more risk.

CHAPTER 23

Money-Making Opportunities in Convertible Bonds

*M*any investors could have earned higher returns in some periods, and with less risk, if they had invested in convertible bonds instead of common stocks. A study by Ibbotson Associates, a consulting firm for institutional investors, shows that in the 20 years from 1973 to 1992, convertible bonds provided higher profits than common stocks, with about half as much risk.

According to *Value Line Convertibles,* a publication of Value Line Publishing, Inc., convertible securities recommended by them from 1971 to 1994 provided an average total return (including price appreciation and income) of 21 percent a year. Some mutual funds that invest in convertibles have done well too. For instance, the Davis A Convertible Securities Fund (800-279-0279) had a 29 percent total return in 1996 compared to 23 percent for the S&P 500 index.

Convertible bonds are often overlooked by individual investors because of the hybrid nature of these securities: They are part equity and part bond. Yet the basic principles and terms of convertibles should be as easy to understand as the key concepts of nonconvertible securities.

There are four reasons why convertible bonds often outperform common stocks:

1. They offer the safety of bonds.
2. They pay more income than common stocks.
3. They can be converted into common stock, so they share in the rise of the common stock.

4. Brokerage commissions for bonds are considerably lower than for stocks.

What Is a Convertible Bond?

A *convertible* bond is a bond that can be exchanged for another security, usually the common stock of the issuing company. Typically, no payment is needed to effect conversion other than the surrender of the bond. The conversion privilege normally lasts for the life of the bond though, in a few cases, the number of common stock shares for which the convertible can be exchanged may change during the life of the convertible.

A convertible bond's value is derived from its conversion privilege (relating to the price of the underlying stock) and from the value it commands simply because it is a bond. Its price rises or falls with its conversion value, that is, with a change in the price of the stock, but its price normally will fall no lower than its investment value as an interest-paying bond.

Usually convertible bonds sell at premiums above their conversion and investment values.

Why Buy Convertibles?

Risk-averse investors tend to prefer convertibles over common stocks because they offer several advantages, one of which is greater income. In early 1997, for instance, the average convertible provided a yield of 6.5 percent, while the average dividend-paying stock in the S&P 500 paid less than 2 percent.

Surprisingly, studies (such as the Ibbotson study noted earlier) have shown that convertibles have consistently outperformed common stocks when both income and price appreciation are considered, over periods of five years or more. This is especially noteworthy, because convertibles are relatively low in risk. When the stock market falls, not only do convertibles fall less, but they also provide greater income. When the market rises, convertibles do not normally rise in price as fast as common stock, but if the market rise is slow, the greater income from convertibles often causes the total return from convertibles to equal or exceed the total return from common stocks. Only in a rapidly rising stock market (such as occurred in 1995 and 1996) do convertibles perform worse.

Another feature that appeals to investors in convertibles is that a portfolio of convertibles typically will be less volatile than a portfolio of common stocks. The more up-and-down movement there is in the price of a security, the greater the risk that its market value may be low when you need to sell it. Thus, less volatility means lower risk.

Why Convertibles Are Safer, Yet Can Be More Profitable Than Stocks

Convertibles are lower in risk than stocks for a number of reasons. First, they are a senior security. A company might skip its common stock dividend if earnings decline, but would stop paying bond interest only as a last resort; if interest payments are stopped, bondholders could take control of the company. Second, convertibles almost always pay a higher yield than stocks. The higher yield helps support the price of the bonds even if the price of the stock falls.

Put another way, fairly priced convertibles are always "favorably leveraged." A convertible will be favorably leveraged it if rises more on a rise in the underlying stock than it falls on a decline in the stock. Convertibles are favorably leveraged because they participate in a rise in the stock, but their higher yields limit the extent of any drop.

Convertible Bond Terms You Should Understand

- *Conversion ratio* is the number of shares of stock for which the convertible can be exchanged. Only the holder of a convertible may convert the issue. The issuing company cannot require the holder to convert nor can it convert the bond for the holder.
- *Conversion value* is the value of a convertible bond if converted into the common stock; it is the price of the common stock multiplied by the bond's conversion ratio. Thus, if you own a bond with a conversion ratio of 25, it is convertible into 25 shares of common stock. If the stock has a market value of $50, the conversion value of your bond is $1,250 (25 × $50).
- *Premium over conversion value* is the percentage by which the price of the convertible bond exceeds the conversion value. For instance, if the price of the convertible is $1,500 and the conver-

sion value is $1,250, the premium over the conversion value is 20 percent.

- *Investment value* is the price at which the convertible would likely trade if it were not convertible, that is, the price at which a "straight" (nonconvertible) bond would trade.
- *Premium over investment value* is the percentage by which the price of the convertible bond exceeds its investment value. For instance, if a convertible bond's price is $1,500 and its investment value (the value the bond would have if it had no conversion feature) is $750, the premium over investment value is 100 percent.
- *Call price* is the price at which the convertible may be called if it is callable. When an issue is called, holders have about 30 days to decide whether to convert. A callable bond is one in which the issuing company has the right to redeem the bond prior to maturity. Bonds are most likely called when interest rates decline and conditions are favorable to the issuer.
- *Call protection* means that, from the date of issue, a bond is protected from being called for a period of one or more years. Most convertible bonds are issued with call protection. If you plan to live off the income from a bond or want to hold it for a specific number of years, you should be sure you have call protection because, without it, your bond could be redeemed by the issuer.
- *Coupon* is the interest payment on a bond. Bonds are nearly always issued with a par value of $1,000, the price at which they will be redeemed at maturity. Thus, a bond with a 9 percent coupon pays $90 in interest per year.
- *Eurobonds* are bonds that were originally sold overseas, usually by U.S. companies. They trade and pay interest in U.S. dollars. Eurobond interest is usually paid once a year versus domestically issued bonds, which pay twice a year.

How to Evaluate Convertibles for Profitability

Corporations issue convertible bonds to raise money. Just like any debt instrument, the issuing company is required to pay the coupon rate and repay the face amount at maturity. An exception is the zero-coupon bond, which pays no cash interest, but instead is issued at a discount from the face value, which reflects the accumulation of interest to maturity equal to the stated original yield to maturity.

One distinct feature convertible bonds offer investors is the ability to exchange the bond for the common stock of the issuing company at the holder's option, allowing the investor to participate in the potential appreciation of the underlying common stock while usually receiving a higher yield than the common dividend pays.

Estimating a convertible bond's fair value and determining whether it is currently overvalued or undervalued requires careful consideration of all its features, including the bond's market price, its investment value, its conversion ratio, its conversion value, the price of the underlying common stock, the bond's call price, the premium over conversion value, and the premium over investment value.

A convertible bond's value is drawn both from its conversion privilege and from the value it commands because it's a bond. As its price rises with its conversion value (that is, with a rise in the underlying stock), its price normally will fall no lower than its investment value. Most often, convertibles sell at premiums above both their conversion and investment values. If, on occasion, you are able to buy a convertible at its investment value, you get the conversion privilege free of cost. And if you are able to buy a convertible at its conversion value, you get the investment feature (better quality and generally higher income) free of cost.

An Information Source for Convertible Bond Investing

If you are interested in looking more closely at the investment opportunities available in convertible bonds, consider using *Value Line Convertibles,* a service published by Value Line Publishing, Inc., 220 East 42nd Street, New York, NY 10017-5891; 800-833-0046. The service provides detailed coverage of more than 500 convertibles, with recommendations, analyses, and performance data. An eight-week trial subscription is available.

A Smart Way to Buy Convertible Bonds

A number of mutual funds invest mainly in convertible securities. Such funds seek high income and capital appreciation by investing a diversified portfolio of bonds, preferred stocks, and other securities that are convertible into common stocks. By investing in mutual funds, you automatically obtain professional management, diversification, and low cost to invest.

Invest the Smart Way

Convertible bonds offer higher yields, with less risk, than investments in common stocks. Convertibles provide the safety of bonds, pay more income than common stocks, and can be converted into common stock, so they share in the potential rise of the common stock.

CHAPTER 24

Growing Your Money with Zero-Coupon Bonds

Zero-coupon bonds (zeros) don't pay out a stream of interest payments like other debt instruments. Instead, they are issued at deep discounts and accumulate and compound the interest. At maturity, the full face amount is paid. Zero-coupon securities offer two main attractions for the investor:

1. Because of the deep discount, they can be bought at very low prices.
2. The guesswork is removed from interest reinvestment, because the yield to maturity is locked in.

Unless you are used to thinking in terms of compound interest over long periods, the mathematical effects of a zero-coupon bond can seem astonishing. For instance, a $1,000 face amount U.S. government zero-coupon bond, maturing in 30 years that has a 7 percent interest rate, could be bought today for just $131. At 7 percent, a zero-coupon bond investment will double in 10 years, triple in 15 years, quadruple in 19 years, and quintuple in 22 years!

Zero-coupon bonds have important disadvantages:

- Income taxes are payable as interest accrues and, because no current income is derived from the zeros, must come from a different source.
- The value of zero-coupon bonds tends to be highly volatile.

- Credit risk of corporate and municipal zeros can be greater than with regular bonds; if an issuer defaults along the way, you will have more to lose because you have not yet received any interest.
- Inflation can erode the value of the bond at maturity.

When to Use Zero-Coupon Bonds

Taxable zeros are widely purchased for inclusion in tax-deferred accounts, such as IRAs and 401(k) plans. Tax-free zeros are a convenient way for high-tax bracket investors to meet future goals. They get an after-tax benefit from the lower interest rates of tax-free securities. Zeros often have attractive yields and are normally held until maturity. Their appeal is a lock-in interest rate as opposed to a yield that varies with the reinvestment value of periodic interest payments in a changing market. If you need to sell a zero prior to maturity, like other fixed-income investments, the value will fluctuate inversely with interest rates. If interest rates decline, the value of your zero-coupon bond will rise, and if interest rates rise, it will fall.

Types of Zero-Coupon Securities

- *Corporate zero-coupon bonds* are issued by corporations and are not usually recommended for individual investors because of the risk of default and because the yield tends not to be competitive in relation to the risk.
- *Strips* are U.S. Treasury or municipal instruments that brokerage firms have separated (stripped) into principal and interest components that are marketed as zero-coupon securities under proprietary acronyms like Salomon Brothers' CATS (certificates of accrual on treasury securities) and M-CATS (certificates of accrual on tax-exempt securities). These securities are represented by certificates with the actual securities being held in escrow. The escrow feature ensures a high degree of security, although the broker is the actual obligor.
- STRIPS (Separate trading of registered interest and principal of securities), the Treasury's acronym for its own zero-coupon securities, are Treasury bonds issued in the traditional way but separated into interest and principal components at the discretion of bondholders using book entry accounts at Federal Reserve Banks.

As direct obligations of the U.S. government, STRIPS are free of credit risk altogether.

- *Municipal zero-coupon securities* are issued by state and local governments and usually are exempt from federal taxes and state taxes in the state of issue. Municipal zeros provide a convenient way to provide for the goals of high-tax-bracket investors who get an after-tax benefit from the lower interest rates of municipals.
- *Zero-coupon convertibles* are a fairly recent development. Introduced in the 1980s, these securities come in two types. One is convertible into common stock providing growth potential. The other, generally a municipal bond, converts into an interest-paying bond, enabling the holder to lock in a rate of accruing interest, and then, 15 years later, to begin collecting interest payments.

Safety Considerations

The safety of corporate and municipal bonds, unless insured, varies with the credit of the issuer, so it is important to check credit ratings. Treasury issues that are stripped (separated into principal and interest components) by brokerage houses and marketed separately as zero-coupon securities are safe as long as the broker holds the underlying Treasury securities in escrow, as is generally done. Some municipal strips, such as M-CATS, are indirectly backed by the U.S. government, because they represent prerefunding invested in Treasury securities. STRIPS, issued directly by the U.S. Treasury are free of any credit risk. Of course, any zero sold in the secondary market prior to maturity is subject to market value fluctuation (interest rate risk).

Invest the Smart Way

You can buy zero-coupon bonds at deep discounts from their face values. Instead of paying out their fixed rate of interest like other debt securities, interest is accumulated and compounded, so you don't have to worry about interest reinvestment. But beware of disadvantages, including current taxability of interest even though it is not being paid out. Also, the market value of zeros tends to be highly volatile.

CHAPTER 25

How to Buy U.S. Treasury Securities Directly

*I*t's a lot easier than you think to buy U.S. Treasury securities, the safest investments money can buy. These securities are direct obligations of the U.S. government. Contrary to what your banker or broker might tell you, buying Treasury bills, notes, or bonds directly from the Federal Reserve is easy. And you can invest in treasury securities without paying any commissions, fees, or other charges through a system called "Treasury Direct."

The U.S. Treasury issues three types of marketable securities: bills, notes, and bonds. (For a description of each, see Chapter 20.) When originally issued, treasuries are sold through an auction process. They are referred to as marketable securities because after their original issue they are bought and sold in the secondary (commercial) market at prevailing market prices through financial institutions, brokers, and dealers in investment securities. Marketable treasury securities are issued only in book-entry form at original issue. Book-entry securities are represented by accounting entries maintained electronically on the records of the U.S. Treasury, a Federal Reserve Bank or branch, or financial institution. Certificates are no longer offered at original issue.

Treasury Direct

If you elect to invest in T-bills, T-notes, or T-bonds by using the Treasury Direct Book-Entry Security System, you may purchase the securities at original issue through any Federal Reserve Bank or branch. The Treasury Direct system is designed primarily for investors who plan to retain their securities from the issue date to maturity. However, you may arrange through a bank or brokerage firm for your investment to be sold before maturity. This is done by requesting that your securities held in the Treasury Direct system be transferred to the commercial system. Your request must be made at least 20 days before an interest payment date or the maturity date of the security.

Figure 25.1, on page 159, lists the 37 Treasury Direct servicing offices at the Federal Reserve Banks and branches, and the Bureau of the Public Debt, where you can purchase treasury securities. You can make your transactions in person or by mail.

You can establish a single Treasury Direct account for all eligible marketable treasury securities. You will receive a statement of account in Treasury Direct after setting up an account, and whenever transactions occur within your account. Principal and interest payments from a Treasury Direct account are paid electronically by direct deposit into your account in a locally authorized bank or other financial institution.

Offering Schedule of Treasuries

Bills

Three series of T-bills are offered on a regular basis. Two series of bills, one having a 13-week term and the other a 26-week term, are offered each week. Unless holidays or special situations occur, the pattern of weekly bill issues is as follows:

1. The offering is announced on Tuesday.
2. The bills are auctioned the following Monday.
3. The bills are issued on the Thursday following the auction.

Bills with a 52-week term are usually offered every four weeks as follows:

1. The offering is announced on Friday.
2. The bills are auctioned the following Thursday.
3. The bills are issued on the Thursday following the auction.

When a normal auction date is a holiday, the auction may be held on the business day preceding or following the holiday.

Notes and Bonds

Though the schedule for the sale of notes and bonds may vary, the U.S. Treasury generally observes the following schedule:

1. Two-year notes and five-year notes are issued on the last business day of each month.
2. Three-year notes and ten-year notes are issued every three months on the 15th of February, May, August, and November.
3. Thirty-year bonds are issued on the 15th of February and August.

Announcements of all offerings of original issue are made through press releases and carried in major newspapers and wire services.

Bill Sales Procedures

The minimum dollar amount acceptable for a tender (application) for T-bills is $10,000. Tenders for more than $10,000 must be in multiples of $1,000. Tenders may be submitted competitively or noncompetitively. Competitive bidders must submit tenders on a discount rate basis with two decimals, such as 4.25 percent. Common fractions may not be used. Competitive bidders may have their bids rejected or may pay a higher price for the security than the noncompetitive price. If you are interested in being a competitive bidder, contact one of the Federal Reserve servicing offices listed in Figure 25.1 for further information.

If, like most investors, you submit a noncompetitive bid, you agree to pay the price equivalent to the weighted discount rate of accepted competitive tenders. In the auction process for bills, all noncompetitive tenders are accepted. Noncompetitive tenders from any single bidder may not exceed $1 million.

The auction results provide information about the range of accepted discount rates and their equivalent prices and investment rates. The discount rate is based on the par value of the bills, while the investment rate is based on the purchase price of the bills and reflects the actual yield to maturity. Both rates are calculated on the actual number of days to maturity. The discount rate is calculated on a 360-day basis (twelve 30-day months). The investment rate is calculated on a 365-day basis.

Note and Bond Sales Procedures

Treasury notes and bonds are sold at a minimum of $1,000 and in multiples of $1,000. The exception is notes with terms of less than four years, which are sold at a minimum of $5,000 and in multiples of $1,000. The specific terms of each new issue, including the minimums available, are provided in the offering announcement. Noncompetitive tenders from any single bidder may not exceed $5 million.

The auction for notes and bonds is done on a yield basis, which means that the competitive bidding is based on the yield the investor is willing to accept on the security. Therefore, if you bid 5.82 percent, it means you will accept an annual yield of 5.82 percent as the return on your investment.

In the auction process for notes and bonds, all noncompetitive tenders are accepted. As in the sale of T-bills, most individual investors submit noncompetitive bids. Competitive bidders may have their bids rejected or may pay a higher price than the noncompetitive price.

When the price of the security is less than par, the investor will receive a discount, which is the difference between the purchase price and par. When the price is over par, the investor will be required to pay a premium, which is also the difference between par and the purchase price. While a discount or premium does affect the return to an investor, it does not affect the stated interest rate the U.S. Treasury will pay investors on an annual basis.

In some cases, the investor is required to pay accrued interest if the security pays interest income for a period prior to the issue date. When the security is announced for sale, the terms will specify if payment of accrued interest is required.

How to Invest through Treasury Direct

To purchase treasury securities through Federal Reserve Banks and branches, you should complete a Treasury Direct tender form. Tender forms are available at any Federal Reserve Bank or branch, or at the Bureau of the Public Debt. They may be obtained by mail or in person. When you submit your tender form by mail, the notation "Tender for Treasury (bill, note, or bond)" should be printed at the bottom of the envelope in which it is sent.

Your tender must be received at the Federal Reserve Bank or branch, or at the Bureau of the Public Debt by the deadline established in the public announcement. Noncompetitive tenders submitted by mail will be considered timely if they are postmarked no later than the day prior to the auction and are received by the issue date.

How to Pay

The tender must be signed and submitted with full payment to the servicing Federal Reserve Bank or branch, or for investors living in the Washington, D.C., metropolitan area, to the Bureau of the Public Debt. Payment may be made in any of the following ways:

- With checks issued by banks, savings and loan associations, or credit unions, or by personal checks (Note: No two-party checks will be accepted. Personal checks submitted in payment for T-bills must be certified.)
- By cash (U.S. currency) presented in person
- By treasury securities maturing on or before the issue date
- By authorizing the Treasury Department to debit the investor's bank account for the exact amount on the day the security is issued

Reinvestment or Redemption

Securities held in Treasury Direct are paid at maturity by direct deposit, unless you have elected to reinvest the proceeds of the maturing securities into new securities.

A request for reinvestment of T-bills, for a period of up to two years, may be made on the tender at the time of original purchase. Reinvestment for notes and bonds held in Treasury Direct are not available at original issue. However, owners of bills, notes, or bonds not scheduled for reinvestment are sent a preredemption notice that shows the eligible securities, if any, into which reinvestments are possible. If you wish to reinvest a security, the notice must be completed and returned by the date specified in the notice. Or, you may reinvest maturing securities by telephone at any hour of the day or night.

Taxation

Treasury securities are subject to all federal taxes, such as income, estate, gift, or excise taxes. However, interest earned on treasury securities is exempt from state and local income taxes. The interest on bills, which are bought with the interest discounted, is taxable in the year in which the bills mature or are sold.

Where to Buy Treasuries

Call, write, or visit in person any of the following 37 Treasury Direct servicing offices located at Federal Reserve Banks and branches, and the Bureau of the Public Debt, throughout the country to obtain a tender. No matter where you are or where you move, you can contact the servicing office nearest you to make transactions and receive information on your account.

FIGURE 25.1   Federal Reserve Banks and Branches

FRB Atlanta 104 Marietta Street Atlanta, GA 30303 404-521-8653	**FRB Charlotte** 530 East Trade Street Charlotte, NC 28230 704-358-2100
FRB Baltimore 502 South Sharp Street Baltimore, MD 21203 410-576-3300	**FRB Chicago** 230 South LaSalle Street Chicago, IL 60690 312-322-5369
FRB Birmingham 1801 Fifth Avenue, North Birmingham, AL 35283-0447 205-731-8708	**FRB Cincinnati** 150 East Fourth Street 513-721-4787 Ext. 334 Cincinnati, OH 45201
FRB Boston 600 Atlantic Avenue Boston, MA 02106 617-973-3810	**FRB Cleveland** 1455 East Sixth Street Cleveland, OH 44101 216-579-2000
FRB Buffalo 160 Delaware Avenue Buffalo, NY 14240-0961 716-849-5000	**FRB Dallas** 2200 North Pearl Street Dallas, TX 75265-5906 214-922-6770

FIGURE 25.1   Federal Reserve Banks and Branches (Continued)

FRB Denver
1020 16th Street
Denver, CO 80217-5228
303-572-2470

FRB Detroit
160 West Fort Street
Detroit, MI 48231
313-964-6157

FRB El Paso
301 East Main
El Paso, TX 79999
915-521-8272

FRB Houston
1701 San Jacinto Street
Houston, TX 77252
713-659-4433

FRB Jacksonville
800-West Water Street
Jacksonville, FL 32231-2499
904-632-1179

FRB Little Rock
325 West Capitol Avenue
Little Rock, AR 72203
501-324-8272

FRB Los Angeles
950 South Grand Avenue
Los Angeles, CA 90051
213-624-7398

FRB Louisville
410 South Fifth Street
Louisville, KY 40232
502-568-9236

FRB Memphis
200 North Main Street
Memphis, TN 38101
901-523-7171 Ext. 423

FRB Miami
9100 NW Thirty-Sixth Street
Miami, FL 33152
305-471-6497

FRB Minneapolis
250 Marquette Avenue
Minneapolis, MN 55480
612-340-2075

FRB Nashville
301 Eighth Avenue, North
Nashville, TN 37203-4407
615-251-7100

FRB New Orleans
525 St. Charles Avenue
New Orleans, LA 70161
504-593-3200

FRB New York
33 Liberty Street
New York, NY 10045
212-720-6619

FRB Oklahoma City
226 Dean A McGee Avenue
Oklahoma City, OK 73125
405-270-8652

FRB Omaha
2201 Farnam Street
Omaha, NE 68102
402-221-5636

FRB Philadelphia
Ten Independence Mall
Philadelphia, PA 19105
215-574-6680

FRB Pittsburgh
717 Grant Street
Pittsburgh, PA 15230-0867
412-261-7802

FIGURE 25.1   Federal Reserve Banks and Branches (Continued)

FRB Portland 915 S.W. Stark Street Portland, OR 97208-3436 503-221-5932	**FRB San Francisco** 101 Market Street San Francisco, CA 94120 415-974-2330
FRB Richmond 701 East Byrd Street Richmond, VA 23261 804-697-8372	**FRB Seattle** 1015 Second Avenue Seattle, WA 98124 206-343-3605
FRB Salt Lake City 120 South State Street Salt Lake City, UT 84130-0780 801-322-7882	**FRB St. Louis** 411 Locust Street St. Louis, MO 63178 314-444-8703
FRB San Antonio 126 East Nueva Street San Antonio, TX 78295 512-978-1303	**Bureau of the Public Debt** 1300 C Street, S.W. Washington, DC 21239-0001 202-874-4000

Invest the Smart Way

You can invest directly in U.S. Treasury securities without paying any commissions, fees, or other charges by setting up a Treasury Direct account. This account will link up with your own bank checking or savings account. Forms you need to set up an account may be obtained by mail or in person at any Federal Reserve Bank or branch.

PART FOUR

Investing the Smart Way in Mutual Funds

CHAPTER 26

The Mutual Fund Phenomenon

*I*n early 1997, some 8,000 mutual funds were managing more than $3.5 trillion. At an increasingly rapid pace, mutual funds have come to have an important and in some ways dominant place in the financial world. They have become the investment of choice for millions of investors, and with good reasons, which will be discussed later.

But where did they start? In a somewhat different form, the origin of modern-day mutual funds dates back to the early 19th century, when they enjoyed substantial popularity in England and Scotland. In the 1820s, "mutuals" reached the United States in the form of a vehicle created by Massachusetts Hospital Life Insurance. Generally balanced between stocks and bonds, a mutual was a load fund managed by professionals and sold by commissioned agents, not unlike today's insurance agents. Many mutuals were sold through plans in which the investor might agree to a $5,000 commitment, paid with $100-a-month installments. About a century later, in 1924, the Massachusetts Investment Trust was organized. It was the first open-end mutual fund and still operates as a member of the Massachusetts Financial Services group in Boston (800-637-2929). During those early years, investment trusts were subject to various abuses and were brought into considerable disrepute. Nonetheless, by 1929, some 525,000 Americans owned shares in them.

Some of today's mutual fund giants were first organized in the 1930s. But the greatest growth of mutual funds occurred after World

War II and has continued to this time with only occasional pauses. In 1946, mutual fund companies managed just over $2 billion in assets. By 1956, this had grown to $10.5 billion and to more than $39 billion in 1966. Growth became sluggish in the 1970s but then exploded in the 1980s. By 1990, 3,000 funds were managing $1 *trillion* in assets; the $2 trillion level was reached—and passed—in 1993, before reaching the $3.5 trillion managed by more than 8,000 mutual funds today. Of this amount, about $1.76 trillion is in stocks. Stock mutual funds now account for 21 percent of the market's total capitalization (up from just 7 percent in 1987). Conservative investors have nearly $1 trillion invested in money-market funds.

What Is a Mutual Fund?

The basic idea of a mutual fund is simple. It is an organization whose only business is the proper investment of its shareholders' money, generally into stocks, bonds, money-market instruments, or a combination of the three, for the purpose of achieving specific investment goals. To do this, it attracts funds from many individual and institutional investors, and it undertakes to invest and manage those funds more effectively than the investors could do on their own.

The ability of a mutual fund to accomplish its goals successfully depends first on how well it can invest a large amount of money into a diversified portfolio of securities that will meet its investment objective. In addition, it must manage its costs efficiently, provide continuous professional management over its extensive investment portfolio, and lastly, provide the many services that mutual fund shareholders have come to expect.

Like other corporations, a mutual fund company issues shares of its own stock. Each share represents the same proportionate interest in the account (portfolio of securities) as every other share. After deduction of necessary expenses, income from the account is distributed to shareholders in the form of dividends. Investment profits and losses are reflected in the value of the shares. Realized profits are distributed to shareholders in the form of capital gains distributions.

One of the great benefits an investor gets by purchasing shares of a mutual fund is that the company's professional investment management and advisory services work for the investor at very low cost.

Open-End and Closed-End Funds

The most common and widely held funds are open-end mutual funds. They have no fixed number of shares outstanding. The number of shares fluctuates from day to day because, for the most part, the funds are constantly selling new shares to investors, and they also stand ready to redeem outstanding shares from investors on any business day.

During a period when investors are buying more shares from a fund than are being redeemed, a cash balance will develop that must be invested, causing the fund to go into the marketplace to purchase securities. On the other hand, when investors are redeeming more shares than are being bought, the fund will be forced to sell securities to make cash available.

The value of an open-end mutual fund share is determined at the end of every business day. This is done by ascertaining the total market value of all the stocks, bonds, and other financial instruments held in the fund, subtracting any liabilities and then dividing the balance by the total number of shares outstanding. This results in the net asset value (NAV) per share. When shares are offered for sale, the buyer will always pay the NAV per share (plus any sales charge that may apply) on the day of his or her purchase. In the same way, when a shareholder tenders shares for redemption, he or she will always receive the NAV per share (less any redemption charges that may apply).

Closed-end funds do not continuously offer new shares for sale, nor do they stand ready to redeem shares from shareowners who wish to sell. Instead, closed-end fund shares are sold in one initial public offering, like the shares of stock in any other corporation. They are then listed for trading on a national securities exchange such as the NYSE. If an investor wishes to buy or sell shares, the investor does so by placing his or her order through a registered securities broker.

While the NAV of closed-end fund shares are calculated in the same way as those of open-end funds, the price an investor will pay or receive for shares traded on an exchange may be above or below the NAV. This is because the price of the shares is determined on an auction market basis, the same as for all other traded shares of stock. Thus, the investor has an additional risk that the owner of open-end funds does not have. The value of a closed-end fund investment is subject not only to the fluctuations of the underlying securities in the fund itself but also to the fluctuating price of the shares on the exchange.

Managers of a closed-end fund have an advantage over their open-end peers, however. Because they do not have to worry about the uneven flow of money going in and out of open-end funds (resulting from share purchases and redemptions), their investment management decisions can be based entirely on economic and market conditions.

Characteristics of a Successful Mutual Fund

A fund whose shares you are considering to purchase should have the following five characteristics:

1. Performance is a mutual fund's reason for being—it should be the driving force behind everything it does, and the fund should pursue it tenaciously.
2. A fund should do what it says. Every mutual fund has a stated objective and a stated strategy for pursuing that objective. It must have the discipline to stick to all that has been stated in its prospectus. This is important because a mutual fund should be only part of your broad financial plan. For your plan to be successful, all its parts must perform.
3. Responsibility for a fund's performance rests with the portfolio manager. This accountability is a powerful incentive. The manager should embrace a disciplined, collaborative approach to investing, where insights and expertise are shared.
4. There is a difference between risk and risky. Risk is a natural, necessary part of investing. It is the engine that drives reward. Well-managed risk helps you achieve your goals. The best mutual funds identify and manage risk, delivering the right balance of risk and reward.
5. Investing with a mutual fund should be easy and the mutual fund company itself should be easy to work with. Communications should be honest, accurate, and easy to understand.

Invest the Smart Way

*M*utual funds attract money from many individual and institutional investors, and undertake to invest and manage those funds more effectively than the investors could do on their own. To accomplish its goals successfully, a fund must invest large amounts of money into a diversified portfolio of securities that will meet its investment objective. Also, it must manage its costs efficiently and provide continuous professional management over its extensive investment portfolio.

CHAPTER 27

Buying Mutual Funds the Way the Pros Do

*I*magine walking into your bank to buy a certificate of deposit and being told there will be a 4 percent sales charge. Your reaction might be, "You mean I have to pay you 4 percent for the privilege of putting my money in your bank—for you to make money on?" Banks don't do this (although they do charge stiff penalties for early withdrawals); but many mutual funds have been charging fees for years. Such a fee is called a *load* or *sales charge* and it's totally unnecessary for you to pay it.

The only reason for a mutual fund to levy a load is to cover its costs of distribution. Most of the charge (about 85 percent) goes to the broker-dealer who handles the sale. The other 15 percent stays with the mutual fund's own sales arm.

The pros don't play this game. They buy directly from the fund and pay no commissions to anyone. You should do the same, and this chapter will show you how.

Buying Mutual Funds without a Broker and without Commissions

One of the great opportunities available to investors today is the ability to buy into diversified, professionally managed portfolios of stocks and bonds at no cost. This is easily done by investing in *no-load* mutual funds. These funds sell their shares directly to the public, with no sales charge.

169

An increasing number of top-rated and well-known mutual funds are no-load funds. Over 800 no-load funds are priced daily in the mutual fund sections of the *New York Times,* the *Wall Street Journal,* and other major newspapers. The funds can be purchased on a direct basis and at no cost to investors. There are, of course, expenses and management fees common to both load and no-load funds. These charges, generally small, are discussed in Chapter 31.

Not all no-load funds are as widely known to the general investing public as some load funds, where a sales commission is involved. This is because many people get their information from stock brokers, who quite naturally are reluctant to provide information on mutual funds that pay no commission. However, brokers do serve an important function in giving investment information to those people who either can't or don't want to take the time to become informed on their own.

Now let's take a look at the two principal ways in which open-end mutual funds are marketed.

Load Funds

These are the mutual funds that are normally distributed through investment broker-dealers. Sales charges, which are described in their prospectuses, can run up to 8.5 percent of the dollar amount paid for the mutual fund. The amount of the sales charge is divided, with a small portion usually going to the sales arm of the mutual fund and the main portion going to the broker-dealer. Of the amount going to the broker-dealer, the firm may get roughly 65 percent and the individual broker about 35 percent. Sales charges can be paid at the time of purchase (a front-end load) or when the shares are redeemed (a back-end load). In some cases there may be a small charge at the time of purchase (a low-load) and another charge at redemption.

Mutual fund shares with front-end loads are offered for sale at a price marked up from the net asset value (NAV) by adding the amount of the sales charge. As discussed earlier, the NAV is the value of all assets held in a fund divided by the total number of shares outstanding. The result is called the *offering price.* Newspapers that carry a daily listing of mutual funds sometimes list both the NAV and the offering price. A person buying shares of a fund will pay the offering price; a person selling shares will receive the NAV.

The sales charge on a front-end load fund is usually tiered, with break-points at different dollar purchase amounts. Figure 27.1 is an

FIGURE 27.1 Sample Schedule of Sales Charges

Amount of Purchase (in thousands)	Sales Charge as a Percentage of Offering Price	Net Asset Value
Less than $100	4.50%	4.71%
$100 to less than $250	3.50	3.61
$250 to less than $500	2.60	2.67
$500 to less than $1,000	2.00	2.04
$1,000 to less than $3,000	1.00	1.01
$3,000 to less than $5,000	0.50	0.50
$5,000 and over	0.25	0.25

example of a typical schedule of sales charges for purchasing shares of a front-end load fund, which would appear in its prospectus.

A fairly recent development in the marketing of mutual funds has been the *back-end load* (contingent deferred sales charge). Under this arrangement, shares are purchased at the NAV. The investor pays no fee at the time of purchase. However, the salesperson must be paid, so the investor will pay a deferred sales charge if the shares purchased are redeemed prior to the end of a stipulated holding period. The amount of the charge declines over time until eventually it disappears. There usually are no break-points for large purchases in back-end load funds. Loads are normally applied to the lesser of original share price or current market value.

A typical back-end load fund's structure might assess a 5 percent charge if shares are redeemed within the first year of ownership, and decline by a percentage point in most years thereafter. In the prospectus, early withdrawal charges would appear as shown in Figure 27.2.

It may seem that an investor who holds on to a back-end fund for more than the stipulated holding period avoids any sales cost, but this is not the case. The money to pay sales and other costs of distributing shares is charged against the fund's income in accordance with SEC Rule 12b-1 under the Investment Company Act of 1940.

Rule 12b-1 fees are assessed by many mutual funds, but they are especially burdensome in the case of back-end load funds because such funds must recoup the commissions paid to salespeople. 12b-1 fees may not total more than 1 percent of average net assets annually.

Investors should carefully consider the effect that annual 12b-1 fees will have on their investment returns. In some back-end load mutual funds, the 12b-1 fee disappears after the end of the early withdrawal

FIGURE 27.2   Early Withdrawal Charges

Year after Purchase	Withdrawal Charge
First year	5%
Second year	4
Third year	3
Fourth year	2
Fifth year	2
Sixth year	1
After six years	0

period, but in most cases the fee continues indefinitely. The fee can have a dramatically negative impact on a fund's long-term total return. For example, consider two funds that are each invested in a portfolio of corporate bonds and produce an average income yield of 7 percent. One fund pays out the full net income to its shareholders, providing them with a distribution rate of 7 percent. The other fund, a back-end load fund with the same 1 percent expense ratio but charging a 1 percent 12b-1 fee, is able to provide its shareholders with a dividend distribution rate of only 6 percent.

No-Load Funds

These funds do not impose any sales charges. You can buy their shares directly from the fund without using a broker and without paying a commission. All other things being equal (investment performance, operating expenses, various fees, investor services, etc.), you can save a great deal of money and increase your investment return significantly by investing in no-load funds.

Mutual fund listings in major daily newspapers often indicate the fee and sales charge policies that apply to individual funds. Typically, an identifying letter is placed next to each fund name where marketing charges apply, as follows:

Symbol	Explanation
a	Fee covering marketing costs is paid from fund assets
d	Deferred sales charge or a redemption fee applies
f	Front-end load applies
m	Multiple fees are charged, usually a marketing fee and either a sales or a redemption fee

In some listings, to indicate a fund is no-load, an *n* will be placed next to the fund name. In other cases, where both NAV and offering prices are shown, *NL* will be inserted in place of the offering price for no-load funds.

In true no-load funds, none of these charges apply. If you are in any doubt about what charges may apply to a particular fund in which you have an interest, just call the fund. Nearly all funds have toll-free numbers. They will be happy to answer your questions and mail you a prospectus.

Because no-load mutual funds sell their shares directly to the public without the use of investment brokers, it is up to the investor to take the initiative by contacting the fund.

Invest the Smart Way

*Y*ou can deal directly with no-load funds without going through a broker, reducing your cost of shares and improving investment results. Most fund companies have toll-free numbers and encourage investors to contact them for information and free literature. Unless there is a particular load fund that you simply must have, I recommend that you steer away from funds that levy sales charges.

CHAPTER 28

Why Big Investors Buy Mutual Funds

*M*ore and more substantial investors are using mutual funds to solve at least some of their investment problems. This trend accelerated with the development of money-market funds in the 1970s. It is no longer unusual for large investors to place multimillion dollar investments in mutual fund accounts. According to the Investment Company Institute, institutional investors alone now account for over 40 percent of all mutual fund assets.

Who are these investors and why do they do it? Many of them certainly can afford to hire their own investment managers on a private basis. Large shareholders of mutual funds today include wealthy individuals, trustees, pensions, profit-sharing and 401(k) retirement plans, corporate funds, endowment funds, and institutions such as churches, schools, and hospitals. In the last analysis, big investors buy mutual funds for many of the same reasons as do small investors.

Performance and Policy

One of the most important reasons why major investors choose mutual funds is the availability of past performance records. No other form of investment management can provide prospective clients with so complete and unquestionable a picture of what it has achieved in the past. The investor can easily see how well any mutual fund manager has handled the funds under his or her care and if those results are suitable to the investor's own investment needs.

Of value, in addition to an accurate picture of past performance, is a mutual fund's clearly stated position relating to objectives, policies, and investment holdings. Not only do mutual fund companies have a wide variety of different objectives and policies, they also provide clear descriptions of exactly what these objectives and policies are and how management goes about implementing them.

Convenience, Simplicity, and Liquidity

For all large investors, the convenience of owning shares in one or a few mutual funds is an important benefit. Contrast this with owning individual shares of stock in many companies, collecting dividends on each, and having to keep records of each transaction. Recordkeeping alone is an important problem that is kept to a minimum by owning mutual funds.

Complete liquidity is another benefit that the large investor appreciates. A portion, or the entire amount, of a mutual fund investment can be liquidated quickly and without any concern about disrupting the market in a particular stock or bond.

Finally, with no-load mutual funds, investors can get money into and out of the market at no cost. There is no commission to buy, no cost to sell (in most cases), and no period of time that the investment must remain in effect. Investors have nearly complete flexibility in the handling of their money. Contrast this with the ownership of individual securities, where an investor must pay a commission to buy and again a commission to sell.

Freedom from Care and Responsibility

Even experienced investors often reach the point where they no longer want the responsibility of managing their own investments. The financial universe has become so large and so complex that it is now virtually impossible for any individual to be competent in all its phases. Other investors simply want the peace of mind that comes from letting someone else do the worrying—managers get paid for it. Many investors have bought a stock that looked attractive, only to watch it immediately drop five or ten points in price. The volatility of such a stock in a mutual fund would hardly be noticed and is probably offset by another stock that is rising.

This brings us to diversification. Large and experienced investors have come to understand and appreciate the benefits of being diversified. Not only can an investor enjoy the advantages of diversification provided by one mutual fund, he or she also can further diversify by spreading assets over several different funds. This provides the additional safety of multiple managers, each of whom is governed by his or her own set of investment objectives and policies. Different managers, objectives, and policies provide varying results in different economic and market climates, further reducing the risks in a large (or small) account.

Trust Accounts

Mutual fund shares have become increasingly accepted as prudent investments for trust accounts and by the banks and trust companies that manage them. This has been especially true with the advent of money-market funds and with the growing acceptance of common stocks as suitable investments for trusts.

The prudent man rule is one that can easily be met by careful selection and investment in mutual funds. This standard was set forth in 1930 by Justice Samuel Putnam in the famous case of *Harvard College v. Amory.* As Justice Putnam stated:

> All that can be required of a trustee . . . is that he shall conduct himself faithfully and exercise a sound discretion. He is to observe how men of prudence, discretion, and intelligence manage their own affairs, not in regard to speculation, but in regard to the permanent disposition of their funds, considering the probable income as well as the probable safety of the capital to be invested . . . .

The purchase of mutual fund shares answers the need for careful selection, adequate diversification, and watchfulness that are essential to prudent investing in stocks and bonds. It is a job that requires continuous diligence. Many trustees, small institutions and individuals alike, simply do not have the time, background, or expertise to undertake this effort. Beyond that, many small trusts do not have sufficient assets to provide the diversification that prudence requires.

Retirement Plans and Institutions

For pension, 401(k), and profit-sharing plans, mutual funds offer various advantages. The fiduciary responsibilities implicit in these plans are similar to those faced by the trustees of personal trusts. By using mutual funds, corporate officers maintain control of the plans while meeting the fiduciary requirements of trustees. They can obtain the particular investment objectives and policies that are suitable for their plans while meeting Internal Revenue Service requirements for maintaining the plans' tax-exempt status.

A further advantage to retirement plans is the ease with which mutual fund investments can be evaluated for performance on an annual, or more frequent, basis. This can be difficult to accomplish for a plan that is invested in a variety of individual stocks and bonds. It is also simple to determine the value of a withdrawing participant's account and to reallocate any forfeited amounts among remaining participants.

Further simplifying the problems of setting up retirement plans is the availability of prototype pension, 401(k), and profit-sharing plans that have been developed by many mutual fund organizations. This makes it unnecessary for companies to devote the time and expense of having their own individual plans drawn up. Individual retirement accounts and retirement plans for self-employed individuals are also offered by most mutual fund groups.

Among the largest investors in the shares of mutual funds are schools, colleges, foundations, hospitals, religious organizations, libraries, unions, and fraternal associations. Such institutions often do not have qualified personnel to handle the proper investment of their funds. But even when they do, they often find it more convenient and prudent to utilize mutual funds for the same reasons that other large investors find advantageous—namely, diversification, investment management, and defined investment objectives and policies.

Invest the Smart Way

*L*arge investors utilize mutual funds for many of the same reasons as do small investors. By experience, they have found that mutual funds provide the benefits they seek in a more cost-effective and convenient way than would otherwise be possible. Here are some key advantages of mutual funds:

- Past performance is easily evaluated.
- Investment objectives and policies are clearly spelled out.
- A diversified portfolio of investments can be set up quickly and at no cost.
- Accounts can be readily liquidated without disrupting the market.
- Investors are relieved of the responsibility and care of managing their investments.

CHAPTER 29

The Wide World of Mutual Funds

Choosing from among the available mutual fund offerings can be daunting. By 1997 more than 8,000 mutual funds were being actively sold in the United States, with wide variances in size, age, purpose, and policy. The oldest have been in existence for over 65 years; many have been established within the past ten years. Some have only several million dollars under management, while others measure their assets in the billions. Obviously, no one fund can serve all investment purposes. The wide appeal of mutual funds depends in large part on the extensive diversity of types that are available.

One investor may seek the greatest potential for capital appreciation. Another may want a high level of current income, or to find a way to reduce income taxes. Others seek to offset the effects of inflation by maintaining the purchasing power of their assets or developing an income that will gradually increase over the years. With all this, most investors also are intensely interested in avoiding the loss of capital.

Each mutual fund is established with clearly stated investment objectives and management policies. These are set forth in the prospectus, which every investor must be given before purchasing shares in a fund. For example, the prospectus of one large money-market fund states that its investment objective is to provide as high a level of current income as is consistent with the preservation of capital and the maintenance of liquidity. To achieve this goal, it describes the types of securities in which it will invest, states that it may seek to enhance yield through lending and borrowing practices, and indicates that it may operate in the futures markets.

As an investor you should recognize that, to achieve a particular objective, a fund manager may have to engage in certain investment practices that involve an increased amount of risk and can result in an impairment of capital under adverse market conditions. The prospectus will spell out the types of risk that are present in connection with the stated investment policies.

The Pitfalls of Statistics

Published total returns of mutual funds can be misleading, as is illustrated by the performance of the Van Wagoner Emerging Growth Fund in 1996. Few newly established mutual funds enjoyed a better year *for management*. Its early success attracted wide media attention, which in turn resulted in enormous amounts of investor dollars pouring into the fund (and millions of dollars in management fees). But as investors came in, the fund's performance deteriorated.

On April 1, 1996, the fund's total year-to-date return was +30.3 percent, on July 1 it was +49.7 percent, and on October 1 it was +42.4 percent. If you had bought shares at the fund's inception on January 1, 1996, and held them until the end of the year, your total return would have been +26.9 percent. So far so good.

However, most investors came in after the first quarter as a result of positive publicity. An investor who bought shares at the beginning of the second, third, or fourth quarter and held them until the end of the year lost money. Because most of the fund's investors bought their shares in the second quarter, most lost money, and the fund had an overall loss to investors for the year. For instance, investors who bought shares on April 1 had a loss of 2.6 percent at the end of the year. Shares bought on July 1 showed a loss of 15.2 percent, and shares bought on October 1 lost 10.9 percent by year-end. At the end of February, 1997, the fund was down an additional 15.4 percent.

If you check only year-to-date or one-year total returns, it is easy to miss signals that a fund's performance has tailed off. Following are some measures you can take to avoid surprises:

- Look for the table titled "statement of operations" in the fund's semiannual report to shareholders and read down to the line labeled "net increase or decrease in net assets from operations." That number is how much the fund has made or lost for investors.

- Check your newspaper. The *New York Times,* for instance, runs three-month and four-week total returns in its mutual fund tables on Thursday and Friday, respectively. Funds that show strong year-to-date gains might be slipping in the short run.
- The fund's net asset value (NAV) can be tracked much like a company's stock price. The NAV at which you purchased shares provides a base from which to chart your fund's performance. But be alert to distributions of dividends and capital gains, which lower NAV but do not affect performance.
- Many newspapers publish weekly summaries of fund performance by classification. Watch for variations between your fund's performance and its group's. But don't let short-term blips obscure your long-term goals.

Types of Mutual Funds

The evaluation of standard investment objectives for the purpose of grouping mutual funds into categories is a matter of judgment based on the information provided in the policy statement found in each fund's prospectus. Most commonly used investment objective classifications are as follows:

- *Adjustable-rate preferred fund.* Invests primarily in adjustable-rate preferred stock
- *Balanced fund.* Primary objective is to conserve principal by maintaining at all times a 60/40 or so ratio of stocks to bonds
- *Canadian fund.* Invests primarily in securities traded in Canadian markets
- *Capital appreciation fund.* Seeks maximum capital appreciation, often by using leverage, heavy portfolio turnover, unregistered securities, options, etc.
- *Convertible securities fund.* Invests its portfolio primarily in convertible bonds and convertible preferred stocks
- *Corporate bond fund.* Invests primarily in corporate bonds; fund also may hold government bonds
- *Emerging markets fund.* Puts at least 65 percent of its assets in equities of foreign emerging markets
- *Equity income fund.* Looks for relatively high current income and growth of income by investing in equities offering these characteristics

- *Environmental fund.* Invests at least 65 percent of its assets in companies contributing to a cleaner and healthier environment, such as waste-management firms
- *European region fund.* Focuses on one or several European stock market(s)
- *Financial services fund.* Invests 65 percent of its assets in stocks of financial service companies, including banks, finance companies, insurers and securities brokerage firms
- *Fixed income fund.* Typically has more than 75 percent of its assets in fixed-income securities, such as bonds, preferred stocks, and money-market instruments
- *Flexible fund.* Aims for high total return by allocating its portfolio among a wide range of asset classes
- *Global fund.* Invests at least 25 percent of its assets in non–U.S. securities
- *GNMA fund.* Invests primarily in Government National Mortgage Association (GNMA) securities
- *Growth and income fund.* Invests in companies expected to enjoy long-term earnings growth and that also pass along some of these earnings in dividend increases
- *Growth fund.* Invests in companies whose long-term earnings are expected to grow faster than the stocks making up the major market indexes
- *Health/biotechnology fund.* Invests primarily in companies engaged in health care, medicine, and biotechnology
- *High-current-yield fund.* Seeks high current yield from fixed-income securities; tends to invest in lower-quality bonds
- *Income fund.* Seeks high current income by investing primarily in bonds and preferred stocks
- *International fund.* Invests in securities that trade primarily outside the United States
- *Japanese fund.* Focuses on securities traded in Tokyo
- *Latin America fund.* Invests primarily in securities in Mexico, Brazil, Chile, and other Latin American countries
- *Mid-cap fund.* Invests in companies with market caps or revenues between $800 million and the average market cap of the Wilshire 4500 index
- *Municipal bond fund.* Invests in the tax-exempt obligations of states, their agencies and municipalities
- *Natural resource fund.* Usually has over 65 percent of its equity holdings in natural-resource stocks

- *Option growth fund.* Seeks to increase its net asset value by investing a portion of its portfolio in options
- *Option income fund.* Writes covered options on a substantial portion of its portfolio to increase income
- *Pacific region fund.* Concentrates on stocks trading in one or more of the Pacific Basin markets
- *Precious metals fund.* Invests primarily in the shares of companies engaged in mining, processing, or owning gold, silver, and other precious metals
- *Preferred stock fund.* Invests primarily in shares of preferred stock
- *Real estate fund.* Puts 65 percent of its assets into real estate securities
- *S&P 500 index fund.* Designed to replicate the performance of the S&P 500 index on a reinvested basis; passively managed, with adviser fee no higher than 0.5 percent
- *Science and technology fund.* Invests primarily in the shares of science and technology stocks
- *Small-company growth fund.* Limits its investments to shares of stock in companies based on size, as described in the prospectus
- *Specialty fund.* Invests in the shares of companies in a specific industry or geographical area
- *U.S. government fund.* Invests in securities issued by the U.S government and its agencies
- *Utility fund.* Invests primarily in shares of stock issued by public utility companies
- *World fixed-income fund*—May own common and preferred stock, but invests primarily in U.S. and foreign debt obligations

This listing, which is by no means all-inclusive, gives an idea of the types of groupings investors may see when they look at reference material or in newspapers and popular financial magazines such as *Barron's, Business Week, Forbes,* and *Money.*

Invest the Smart Way

With over 8,000 mutual funds being actively sold in the United States, choosing from among them for your own portfolio can be daunting. Obviously, no one fund can serve all investment purposes. Each fund is established with clearly stated investment objectives and management policies.

CHAPTER 30

Why a Prospectus?

*P*erhaps the most important source of information afforded mutual fund investors is the prospectus. The law stipulates that the offering of any mutual fund for sale to the public must be accompanied or preceded by a prospectus. Prospectuses generally must be updated at least annually.

A prospectus sets forth concisely the information that a prospective investor should know about a specific mutual fund before investing. For more detailed information, a statement of additional information may be obtained without charge by writing or calling the mutual fund company. (Use their toll-free line.) The statement, which is incorporated by reference into the prospectus, has been filed with the Securities and Exchange Commission (SEC). Each prospectus also is required to display prominently the following words: "These securities have not been approved or disapproved by the Securities and Exchange Commission or any state securities commission nor has the Securities and Exchange Commission or any state securities commission passed upon the accuracy or adequacy of this prospectus. Any representation to the contrary is a criminal offense."

Before permitting a mutual fund company to offer a fund for sale to the public, the SEC examines the statement of additional information to be sure it contains all the information required by law. When that requirement has been met, the fund company is notified that it may offer its fund for sale to the public.

For illustration purposes, we'll look at the 1996 prospectus of the T. Rowe Price Blue Chip Growth Fund (a stock fund seeking long-term capital growth). This same type of data will be found in the prospectuses of most mutual funds.

What the Prospectus Contains

Investment Objectives

The first page of the 1996 prospectus of the T. Rowe Price Blue Chip Growth Fund sets forth in typical fashion the investment objective of the fund. It states that the fund's goal is "To provide long-term growth. Income is a secondary consideration." As with any mutual fund, there is no guarantee the fund will achieve its goal.

Here are a few examples of the investment objectives you are likely to find in the prospectuses of other types of mutual funds:

- *Money-market fund.* To provide maximum current income consistent with the preservation of capital and the maintenance of liquidity
- *Global equity fund.* To earn a high level of total return through investments in the various capital markets of the world
- *Balanced fund.* To strive for the balanced accomplishment of three investment objectives—income, capital growth, and stability
- *Government securities fund.* To realize high current income consistent with reasonable safety of principal by investing in obligations issued or guaranteed by the U.S. Treasury or by various agencies of the U.S. government
- *Long-term municipal bond fund.* To seek as high a level of interest income exempt from federal income tax as is consistent with the preservation of capital

Investment Policies

In the investment policies section of a prospectus, each fund spells out the types of securities—stock, bond, or money market—it invests in to achieve its objective. This section of the prospectus will also identify in general terms the investment grade or quality of that type of security, the kind of organization that issues it, and the types of transactions and investment techniques the fund uses in pursuing its objective.

FIGURE 30.1   Example of Expenses from a Typical No-Load Mutual Fund Prospectus

Shareholder Transaction Expenses	
Sales Load Imposed on Purchases	None
Sales Load Imposed on Reinvested Distributions	None
Redemption Fees*	None
Exchange Fees	None
Annual Fund Expenses	
Management Fee	0.61 %
12b-1 Marketing Fees	None
Other Expenses (Custodial, Auditing, etc.)	0.35
Total Operating Expenses (Expense Ratio)	**0.96 %**

*Some funds may charge a small transaction fee (say, 1 percent) on redemptions of shares that have been held less than one year.

The investment policy of the T. Rowe Price Blue Chip Growth Fund is to invest at least 65 percent of total assets in the common stocks of large and medium-sized blue chip companies. These companies will be well-established in their industries and have the potential for above-average growth in earnings. Most of the assets will be invested in U.S. common stocks. However, the fund also may purchase other types of securities, for example, foreign securities, convertible stocks and bonds, and warrants, when considered consistent with the fund's investment objective and program.

Fund Expenses

The prospectus of each fund includes a table near the front that illustrates all the expenses and fees a shareholder of the fund incurs. Shareholder transaction expenses may include a sales load imposed on purchases, a sales load imposed on reinvested dividends, redemption fees, and exchange fees. In the case of most true no-load funds, there are no charges for any of these activities. Other funds will indicate their charges as a percentage of net asset value (NAV) or dollar amount. See Figure 30.1 for an example of how a typical no-load fund prospectus sets forth its charges.

Financial Highlights Table

Mutual fund prospectuses provide a financial highlights table with selected per-share data and ratios. This table is also located near the front of the prospectus. It gives information about how the fund is doing with money you've invested. It shows what you would have earned, in dividends and capital gains distributions, on one share for each year indicated. It also shows any increase or decrease in the value of that share during the year. Funds are required to show these results for each of the past ten years, or if the fund is less than ten years old, for each year it has been in existence.

Investment Risks

Every prospectus points out that, like any investment program, a mutual fund entails certain risks. A fund investing in common stocks is subject to stock market risk—that is, the possibility that stock prices in general will decline over short or even extended periods. The stock market tends to be cyclical, with periods when stock prices generally rise or decline.

The T. Rowe Price Blue Chip Growth Fund prospectus warns that growth stocks can be volatile for several reasons: Because they usually reinvest a high portion of earnings in their own businesses, they may lack the dividend yield associated with value stocks that can cushion total return in a declining market. Also, because investors buy these stocks because of their expected superior earnings growth, earnings disappointments often result in sharp price declines.

Investment results for several periods throughout a fund's lifetime help an investor see how money invested in a fund has fared in the past. Whenever you see information on a fund's performance, do not consider the figures to be an indication of the performance you could expect by making an investment in the fund today. The past is an imperfect guide to the future; history does not repeat itself in neat, predictable patterns.

Share Price

A mutual fund's share price, called its net asset value, is calculated each business day after the close of regular trading (generally 4:00 P.M. Eastern time) of the New York Stock Exchange.

Daily net asset value is useful to you as a shareholder because, multiplied by the number of fund shares you own, NAV gives you the dollar amount you would have received had you sold all of your shares back to the fund that day. The fund's share price can be found daily in the mutual fund listings of most major newspapers under the heading of the fund's sponsor.

Opening an Account

Each prospectus includes information on how to open an account and purchase shares in the fund and will be accompanied by a new account form. Your purchase must be equal to or greater than the minimum initial investment. For different funds, this may range anywhere from as little as $50 to as much as $50,000 or more. Most funds can be started in the $1,000 to $3,000 range. Fund shares may be purchased by mail, by wire, by exchange from another fund in the same family of funds, directly from your checking account, or by other means that will be explained in the prospectus.

When opening a new account, you must select one of three distribution options:

1. *Automatic reinvestment option.* Both dividends and capital gains distributions will be reinvested in additional shares of the fund.
2. *Cash dividend option.* Your dividends will be paid in cash and capital gains will be reinvested in additional fund shares.
3. *All-cash option.* Dividend and capital gains distributions will be paid in cash.

Some funds permit distributions to be reinvested automatically in shares of another fund of the same family.

Other Important Information

The prospectus contains other information that you will find helpful in establishing and maintaining a mutual fund investment.

- *Signature guarantees.* Most funds require that for certain written transaction requests, your signature must be guaranteed by a bank, trust company, or member of a domestic stock exchange. Having a document notarized does not qualify as a signature guarantee.

- *Certificates.* Most funds will issue share certificates on request.
- *Canceling trades.* A trade received by a fund in writing or by telephone, if believed to be authentic, may not normally be canceled. This would include purchases, exchanges, or redemptions.
- *Trade dates.* These are the dates on which accounts are credited. If a purchase or sale is received by 4:00 P.M. (Eastern time), the trade date is the date of receipt. If received after 4:00 P.M., the trade date is the next business day.
- *Exchanges.* Shares can be sold by exchanging into another mutual fund in the same family of funds. It is important to remember that this constitutes a taxable event, and any gain or loss is reportable for income tax purposes. (Many funds charge a small fee—e.g., $5—for exchanges.)
- *Other services.* The prospectus explains special services and options that are available to the investor, such as automatic investment plans, automatic withdrawal plans, telephone services, and so on.

Invest the Smart Way

*T*he prospectus is an important tool for prospective mutual fund investors. A well-written prospectus is easy to read and provides a wealth of essential information, including investment objectives and policies, expenses and fees, historical performance data, a guide on how to open an account, and the various services furnished by the fund.

CHAPTER 31

How to Reduce Your Costs and Increase Your Returns

A little-recognized fact that you as a current or prospective mutual fund investor should realize is that—over time—sales charges, high fees, excessive operating costs, and other expenses can eat into a substantial portion of your investment assets. This chapter explains the basics of mutual fund costs and shows you how to eliminate or reduce much of this waste from your mutual fund portfolio.

The Basics of Mutual Fund Costs

Mutual fund costs fall into two general categories: sales charges (known as "loads") and expenses incurred in the fund's operation. Not all mutual funds charge loads, but all funds have operating expenses that are deducted from fund earnings. Certain types of account fees are also sometimes charged.

Loads

These sales fees fall in three types: front-end loads (the most common), back-end loads, and level loads. Front-end loads are assessed when you purchase fund shares; back-end loads are paid when you redeem (sell) fund shares; level loads are charged annually, buried in other marketing and distribution expenses.

- *Front-end loads* range between 4 percent and 8.5 percent of your investment. This has the effect of reducing the amount you initially invest. For instance, if you invest $10,000 in a fund with a 5 percent load, your net amount invested becomes $9,500. Some funds also charge a load when you reinvest dividends in additional shares.

- *Back-end loads* may either be a percentage of the amount you redeem or a flat fee. A back-end load (deferred sales charge) can impose a fee of 5 percent to 6 percent of the proceeds of any redemption made during the first year. The fee usually decreases by 1 percent per year over a period of five to six years, and then disappears by the seventh year.

- *Level loads* may be as much as 0.75 percent per year on a continuing basis. These charges are deducted each year from fund assets as marketing and distribution costs, paid as commissions to brokers and financial advisers, and reported as part of the fund's expenses. Sometimes these charges are combined with front-end or back-end loads.

Mutual funds that do not have any sales commissions or fees are known as *no-load,* while funds that charge 1 percent to 3 percent of the amount you invest are known as *low-load.*

Operating Expenses

The term *operating expenses* refers to the normal costs a mutual fund incurs in conducting business, including management fees, investment advisory fees, and the expenses associated with fund administrative services such as maintaining offices, staff, and equipment. Called an *expense ratio,* and usually expressed as an annual percentage of the fund's average net assets, these costs may range from under 0.20 percent of a fund's assets (for certain funds of the Vanguard Group and USAA Investment Management Company) to well above 2 percent.

Sometimes a fund's sponsor may temporarily waive its management fee or even absorb *all* operating expenses to enhance the fund's current yield. This is a relatively common practice with new mutual funds in an attempt to attract investors. Be alert for it when comparing fund yields; it probably won't last long.

Expenses are paid by a fund first out of investment income, which is more than sufficient in most cases. An exception would be for funds that invest entirely in growth companies that pay little or no dividends. Then expenses must come out of invested capital.

12b-1 Fees

As discussed earlier, many funds charge an additional fee known as a *12b-1* fee. The term "12b-1" refers to the 1980 Securities and Exchange Commission rule that permits charging marketing and distribution-related expenses directly against the fund's assets. The fund's prospectus outlines 12b-1 fees, if applicable. Rules of the National Association of Securities Dealers have placed two caps on the level of 12b-1 fees. One is an annual limit of 0.75 percent of a fund's assets. An additional 0.25 percent service fee may be paid to brokers or other sales professionals in return for providing ongoing information and assistance to shareholders. There is also a rolling cap on total sales charges, to be calculated at 6.25 percent of new sales plus interest for funds that pay a service fee, and 7.25 percent plus interest for funds that do not pay a service fee.

The term *level load* refers to that portion of 12b-1 fees that is used to compensate brokers and investment advisers for selling shares of the fund. If a fund charges a 12b-1 fee in excess of 0.25 percent, it may not call itself a no-load fund, even if it has no other sales charges. This amount, like all operating expenses, is deducted directly from a fund's earnings.

Account Maintenance Fees

Some funds assess fees on all accounts, usually between $10 and $25 per year. These account maintenance fees are generally charged against accounts that are below (or fall below) a stated dollar amount. This charge is meant to fairly apportion expenses among shareholders, because all fund accounts, regardless of their size, cost about the same to maintain.

Exchange Fees

These charges, typically between $5 and $25, are sometimes assessed when you exchange shares from one fund to another within a fund family.

Transaction Fees

These fees, usually 1 percent or 2 percent, may be assessed on either purchases or redemptions. The charges are not sales loads, because they are not used to compensate salespeople. Rather, transaction fees are paid directly to the fund itself to help defray the costs associated with the purchase and sale of securities.

You should understand that none of these fees (except for investment management and advisory fees) relates in any way to the results attained by the investment management of a fund. Some investors wrongly believe that higher fees equate to better investment management. You can easily determine whether a fund is charging a load, redemption fee, or 12b-1 fee simply by checking the mutual fund listings in most newspapers.

Compare Mutual Fund Costs

Every mutual fund must report its expense charges annually in a consolidated fee table near the front of its prospectus. This makes it very easy for you to compare charges from one fund to another. Of course, expense charges are just one factor to consider in the selection of a fund. But again, other things being equal (management ability, past performance, and investment objectives and policies), a fund with low expenses will tend to produce a better return than will one with charges that are out of line with the competition.

A good example of a fund that keeps its expenses to a minimum is the Vanguard Wellington Fund, a no-load fund and member of the Vanguard Group. Begun in 1929, the Wellington Fund has had a long history of superior performance. It had net assets in excess of $16 billion in early 1997. The information in Figure 31.1 appeared in its 1996 prospectus.

Invest the Smart Way

Mutual funds provide a cost-effective solution for the professional management of your funds. Carefully compare the costs of the mutual funds you consider for purchase, but remember, investment decisions should not be based on costs alone. The fund's performance and your risk tolerance, goals, and time horizon should always come first.

FIGURE 31.1   Sample Expenses from Vanguard Wellington Fund
                 Prospectus

FUND EXPENSES

The following table illustrates all expenses and fees that you would
incur as a shareholder of the Fund. The expenses set forth below
are for the 1995 fiscal year.

Shareholder Transaction Expenses

Sales Load Imposed on Purchases	None
Sales Load Imposed on Reinvented Dividends	None
Redemption Fees	None
Exchange Fees	None

Annual Fund Operating Expenses

Management & Administrative Expenses		0.24%
Investment Advisory Fees		0.05
12b-1 Fees		None
Other Expenses		
Distribution Costs	0.02%	
Miscellaneous Expenses	0.02	
Total Other Expenses		0.04
Total Operating Expenses		**0.33%**

The purpose of this table is to assist you in understanding the various costs and expenses that you would bear directly or indirectly
as an investor in the Fund.

The following example illustrates the expenses that you would incur
on a $1,000 investment over various periods, assuming (1) a 5%
annual rate of return and (2) redemption at the end of each
period. As noted in the table above, the Fund charges no redemption fees of any kind.

1 Year	3 Years	5 Years	10 Years
$3	$11	$19	$42

This example should not be considered a representation of past or
future expenses or performance. Actual expenses may be higher
or lower than those shown.

Source: Reprinted by permission of the Vanguard Group.

CHAPTER 32

Investing for Growth in U.S. Stock Funds

*P*atient investors seeking to build a fortune have been amply rewarded by investing in well-managed mutual funds with an objective of capital appreciation. The concept of investing for the long haul is nowhere more important than for the investor whose investment objective is growth of capital.

There are almost as many individual mutual fund approaches to investing for growth as there are investment managers trying to do it. Each manager tends to develop a personal style, based on his or her concept of how best to achieve the elusive goal of making money grow. For convenience, a limited number of fund classifications are generally recognized, based on broad investment objectives and policies. In many cases a particular fund will not fit neatly into any one of these classifications, so analysts include it in the group they feel it most nearly matches.

Within these fund groupings there are wide individual differences between the funds as to their specific investment objectives and policies, as well as in their investment performance. It is useful, though, to compare the average performance of various categories of funds over a period of time.

Keep in mind that when investing for growth, current income is not a high priority. All numbers in Figure 32.1 reflect total return (price change and income). They assume that income dividends and capital gains distributions have been reinvested into additional shares. The data

FIGURE 32.1   Average Investment Performance of Selected Fund
Groups (Average Annual Total Return for the Period
Ending March 31, 1997)

Mutual Fund Classification	1 Year	5 Years	10 Years
Large Company Growth Funds	11.8%	13.1%	11.2%
Mid-sized Company Stock Funds	5.1	12.7	11.5
Small Company Stock Funds	4.7	13.1	11.2
Specialty Stock Funds	6.2	13.5	10.5
General U.S. Treasury Funds	2.8	6.9	7.9
Corporate Bond Funds	6.8	8.6	8.5
S&P 500 Index	**19.8**	**16.4**	**13.4**

corroborates a basic principle of investing. There is a direct correlation
between risk and reward: The greater the risk, the greater the potential
reward. Funds that invest in common stocks generally have experienced
significantly higher long-term results (see the total return column for ten
years) than have funds that invest primarily in bonds. In the debt-ori-
ented funds, corporate bonds outperformed U.S. Treasury securities.
This would be expected due to the lower risk level of treasuries.

Another interesting fact is that there is frequently an inverse relationship between a fund's current yield and the long-term growth it
realizes. Funds with the lowest average yields (stock funds) produce
the highest long-term returns. Conversely, bond funds produce much
lower long-term returns. Money-market funds, with no risk of market
fluctuation, have the lowest returns.

Next let's look at some specific fund classifications you should consider when investing for growth. I'll describe the objective and investment policies of each and list some of the top-performing no-load funds
in each group. A fund's objective refers to what the fund seeks to
accomplish for its shareholders, while its investment policy sets forth
the means, or management techniques, by which it hopes to attain its
objective. It is important when comparing funds that they are all pursuing the same objective. After all, over time one would expect a small
company growth fund to have a greater total return than a less-risky
large company fund. Although in fact that does not always hold true.

The funds in each group are ranked in order of best average annual
returns for the five years ending on March 31, 1997. This period
included two extraordinary years of stock market performance. In 1995

FIGURE 32.2 Top-Performing Large Company Growth Funds (Average Annual Return for the Period Ending March 31, 1997)

Fund	3 Years	5 Years	Telephone
Legg Mason Value Trust— Primary	27.7%	20.4%	800-822-5544
Safeco Equity No Load	20.8	19.5	800-426-6730
Vanguard Index Trust 500 Portfolio	22.2	16.3	800-662-7447
Harbor Capital Appreciation	20.1	16.2	800-422-1050
Vanguard U.S. Growth	23.3	14.2	800-662-7447

the S&P 500 Composite Stock Index produced a return (including reinvested dividends) of 37.5 percent and in 1996 the index had a total return of 22.9 percent. You can obtain a prospectus and other fund information for each fund shown by calling the telephone number following the listing.

Some excellent funds that are closed to new investors have been omitted from consideration.

Large Company Growth Funds

Funds included in this category generally invest in companies with market capitalizations of $5 billion and up. As a primary objective they usually seek long-term capital appreciation. Often, a secondary objective is growth in income. Investment policies typically include investment in the stock of companies that have favorable earnings and long-term growth prospects.

This group includes many index funds, but a larger number try to beat the S&P 500 with higher returns. Some funds are successfully managed and many others are not. Top-performing no-load large company growth funds are listed in Figure 32.2.

Vanguard Index Trust 500 Portfolio

Minimum initial investment: $3,000
Minimum subsequent investment: $100
Date of inception: August 31, 1976
Load: None

Investment Objective

The fund seeks investment results that correspond with the price and yield performance of the S&P 500 index. The fund allocates the percentage of net assets invested in each company's stock on the basis of the stock's relative total market value: its market price per share multiplied by the number of shares outstanding.

Performance

If you had invested $10,000 for 15 years in Vanguard Index Trust 500 Portfolio on December 1, 1982 (and reinvested income dividends and capital gains), it would have grown to a value of $97,220 on November 30, 1996. The same amount invested for ten years on December 1, 1987, would have had a value of $40,312 on November 30, 1996.

Mid-sized Company Stock Funds

Funds included in this category generally invest in companies with market capitalizations between $1 billion and $5 billion. As a primary objective they usually seek long-term capital appreciation. Often, a secondary objective is growth in income. Investment policies typically permit investment in the stock of companies with smaller market capitalizations. They tend to be diversified among a variety of growth stocks and pay modest dividends. Top-performing no-load mid-sized company stock funds are listed in Figure 32.3.

FIGURE 32.3   Top-Performing Mid-Sized Company Stock Funds (Average Annual Return for the Period Ending March 31, 1997)

Fund	3 Years	5 Years	Telephone
Oakmark	20.5%	23.6%	800-625-6275
PBHG Growth	12.8	21.5	800-809-8008
Mairs & Power Growth	27.4	20.1	800-304-7404
First Eagle Fund of America	18.7	19.1	800-451-3623
Torray	26.2	18.9	800-443-3036

A Recommended Mid-sized Company Stock Fund

Mairs & Power Growth Fund

Minimum initial investment: $2,500
Minimum subsequent investment: $100
Date of inception: November 7, 1958
Load: None

Investment Objective

The fund seeks long-term capital appreciation and invests primarily in common stocks and expects to remain fully invested in stocks at all times, though a portion of the assets may be invested in cash and short-term instruments. The fund seeks companies with reasonably predictable earnings, above average return on equity, market dominance, and financial strength. It normally has a low portfolio turnover rate relative to comparable funds.

Performance

If you had invested $10,000 for 15 years in Mairs & Power Growth Fund on December 1, 1981 (and reinvested income dividends and capital gains), it would have grown to $116,925 on November 30, 1996. The same amount invested for ten years on December 1, 1986, would have had a value of $48,910 on November 30, 1996.

FIGURE 32.4   Top-Performing Small Company Stock Funds (Average Annual Return for the Period Ending March 31, 1997)

Fund	3 Years	5 Years	Telephone
Baron Asset	20.4%	17.7%	800-992-2766
Kaufmann	18.2	16.9	800-666-4943
T. Rowe Price Small Cap	16.6	16.1	800-638-5660
T. Rowe Price OTC Securities	17.3	14.8	800-638-5660
Vanguard Index Small Cap Stock	13.6	13.3	800-662-7447

Small Company Stock Funds

Funds included in the small company category generally invest in companies with market capitalizations less than $1 billion. These funds typically seek out the stocks of small, fast-growing companies, with the potential for strong earnings stemming from favorable sales gains and superior return on invested capital. The stocks they hold frequently pay little or no dividends. Top-performing no-load small company stock funds are listed in Figure 32.4.

A Recommended Small Company Stock Fund

Baron Asset Fund

Minimum initial investment: $2,000
Minimum subsequent investment: None
Date of inception: June 12, 1987
Load: None

Investment Objective

The fund seeks capital appreciation and invests in companies with market capitalizations between $100 million and $1.5 billion that the manager believes have undervalued assets or favorable growth prospects. The fund looks for fundamentals such as strong balance sheets, undervalued and unrecognized assets, low multiples of cash flow and income, perceived management skills, unit growth, and the potential to capitalize on anticipated economic trends.

FIGURE 32.5   Top-Performing Specialized Stock Funds (Average Annual Return for the Period Ending March 31, 1997)

Fund	3 Years	5 Years	Telephone
John Hancock Regional Bank B*	25.1%	25.6%	800-257-3336
Invesco Strategic Financial Services	22.9	20.2	800-930-6300
Cohen & Steers Realty Shares	17.2	19.1	800-437-9912
Midas	6.1	18.9	800-400-6432
Vanguard Specialized Health Care	27.9	18.6	800-662-7447

*These funds have deferred sales fee (loads) of up to 5 percent.

Performance

If you had invested $10,000 for five years in Baron Asset Fund on January 1, 1991 (and reinvested income dividends and capital gains), your fund value would have grown to $24,926 on December 31, 1996.

Specialized Stock Funds

Funds included in the specialized category limit their investments to a specific industry such as retailing, transportation, or paper, or falls outside other classifications. Top-performing specialized stock funds are listed in Figure 32.5.

A Recommended Specialized Stock Fund

Invesco Strategic Financial Services

Minimum initial investment: $1,000
Minimum subsequent investment: $50
Date of inception: June 2, 1986
Load: None

Investment Objective

The fund seeks capital appreciation and normally invests at least 80 percent of assets in the equities of financial services companies, including commercial and industrial banks, savings and loan associations, consumer and industrial finance companies, leasing companies, securities brokerage companies, and insurance companies.

Performance

If you had invested $10,000 for ten years in Invesco Strategic Portfolios Financial Services on February 1, 1987 (and reinvested income dividends and capital gains), it would have grown to $59,832 on January 31, 1997. The same amount invested for five years on February 1, 1992, would have had a value of $25,862 on January 31, 1997.

Invest the Smart Way

*L*ong-term investors with an objective of capital appreciation have been amply rewarded by investing in well-managed mutual funds. The concept of investing for the long haul is critical if you want to grow your capital. It's a rule of thumb that the longer your time horizon, the more risk you can take on. The catch is that many investors panic when they confront that risk in fact rather than in theory.

CHAPTER 33

Making Money in Science and Technology Funds

Some investors write off sector funds as simply high-risk, speculative investments. But, according to the January 1996, *Morningstar Investor,* "They're not only missing out on some super, well-managed funds—they may be robbing themselves of better returns."

Sector funds are convenient ways to invest in segments of the economy that you believe have the growth potential to outperform the general market. As part of a balanced portfolio, sector funds can be as important as any other mutual fund at helping you achieve your goals, such as growing your money, saving for retirement or college, and beating inflation. Sector fund categories include communications; financial; health; natural resources; precious metals; real estate; science and technology; and utilities.

Although past performance is no guarantee of future results, the science and technology sector has been experiencing revolutionary changes and growing with exceptional speed. An incredible pace of innovation in technology products is creating new opportunities for businesses to cut costs and improve productivity as well as providing new sources of information, education, and entertainment to consumers. The dynamic characteristics of the science and technology sector creates growth opportunities for innovative companies, and growth fuels appreciation in stock prices. No-load science and technology funds represent an inexpensive, diversified way to make focused investments in rapidly developing markets.

FIGURE 33.1   Top-Performing Science and Technology Funds
(Average Annual Return for the Period Ending March 31, 1997)

Fund	5 Years	10 Years	Telephone
Fidelity Select Electronics Portfolio*	33.4%	17.1%	800-544-8888
Fidelity Select Computers Portfolio*	25.9	14.4	800-544-8888
T. Rowe Price Science and Technology	21.2	N/A	800-426-6730
Fidelity Select Software and Computer Services Portfolio*	21.1	15.7	800-544-8888
Invesco Strategic Portfolios Technology	18.4	16.1	800-525-8085
Fidelity Select Technology*	20.8	13.5	800-544-8888

*These funds charge a 3 percent load to buy shares.
N/A—This fund has not operated for a full ten years.

In most cases, you should hold a sector fund for at least three years. You invest in a science and technology fund because you believe that sector is in the midst of dynamic change, change that offers opportunity, not just in the months ahead but for several years into the future. Leaders in the industry see unparalleled growth ahead for the next 15 to 20 years. This suggests that your investment time horizon should be just as long. Maintain the same long-term outlook effective with any equity fund investment.

Typically, science and technology funds invest in companies that specialize in computer hardware; computer software and service; electronics and semiconductors; communications equipment and manufacturing, video, electronics, and robotics; and those focused on office and factory automation. These funds look for companies with strong market positions that benefit from using technology and offer new product innovation.

Funds included in the science and technology category are the most growth-driven of all equity funds. They are among the most volatile in the mutual fund universe. Most of the funds' assets are devoted to computer-related technology, though a few also buy shares of drug and biotech companies. Many funds with aggressive growth, small company, and growth objectives also invest heavily in science and technology stocks.

The science and technology group includes several funds in the Fidelity Group, which charge investors a 3 percent load. They are included here because of the small number of funds in the category that have been around long enough to have meaningful performance records. Figure 33.1 reflects the top-performing funds in the science and technology category. The funds are ranked in order of performance for the five years ended March 31, 1997.

A Recommended Science and Technology Fund

T. Rowe Price Science and Technology Fund

Minimum initial investment: $2,500
Minimum subsequent investment: $100
Date of inception: September 30, 1987
Load: None

The fund was ranked first in its category for the period from its inception through December 31, 1996, according to Lipper Analytical Services, which tracked 13 science and technology funds for that period.

Aggressive investors who are looking for significant growth and are willing to accept greater risk in pursuit of their long-term goals should invest in this fund.

Investment Objective

The fund seeks to provide investors with long-term capital growth. Income is not a consideration. The fund invests at least 65 percent of total assets in the common stocks of companies expected to benefit from the development, advancement, and use of science and technology.

Industries likely to be represented in the portfolio include computers and peripheral products; software; electronic components and systems; telecommunications; media and information services; pharmaceuticals; hospital supply and medical devices; biotechnology; environmental services; chemicals and synthetic materials; and defense and aerospace. Investments may also include companies that should benefit from the commercialization of technological advances even if they are not directly involved in research and development.

Most of the assets are invested in U.S. common stocks. However, the fund may also purchase other types of securities, when considered consistent with the fund's investment objective, for example, foreign securities; convertible stocks and bonds; and warrants.

Stock selection is not based on company size but rather on an assessment of the company's fundamental prospects. As a result, holdings range from small companies developing new technologies or pursuing scientific breakthroughs to large, blue-chip firms with established track records or developing and marketing such advances.

Following are the 20 largest common stock holdings of the T. Rowe Price Science and Technology Fund on December 31, 1996.

Company	Percent of Assets	Company	Percent of Assets
BMC Software	5.1%	Xilinx	2.6%
3Com	5.0	Synopsys	2.4
Oracle	4.4	Electronic Data Systems	2.0
Cisco Systems	3.9	ADC Telecommunications	1.9
Intel	3.2	Ascend Communications	1.9
Analog Devices	3.1	Network General	1.7
America Online	3.0	Linear Technology	1.7
Microsoft	3.0	Boston Scientific	1.5
Maxim Integrated Products	3.0	FORE Systems	1.5
First Data	2.8	Shiva	1.5

Performance

The T. Rowe Price Science and Technology Fund had an average annual return of 21.72 percent from its inception in 1987 through the end of 1996. Its rate of return was well in excess of the Lipper Science and Technology Category Average (15.79 percent) and that of the S&P 500 stock index (12.82 percent). If you had invested $10,000 in the fund on September 30, 1987 (when it began operations), with income dividends and capital gains reinvested, your investment would have grown to a value of $61,607 on December 31, 1996. This compares with a growth of $10,000 to $39,858 during the same period in the Lipper Science and Technology Category Average, and to $30,531 in the S&P 500 index.

Remember that while long-term performance is an important aspect of any investment decision, it becomes even more so when considering aggressive growth funds. Although they can produce

FIGURE 33.2   Financial Highlights of T. Rowe Price Science and Technology Fund

Year	NAV	Total Return	Income	Capital Gains	Expense Ratio
1988	8.57	13.27%	$0.07	$0.44	1.20%
1989	10.53	40.67	0.06	1.39	1.20
1990	10.05	−1.33	0.09	0.24	1.25
1991	15.57	60.17	0.00	0.48	1.25
1992	17.33	18.76	0.00	1.12	1.25
1993	18.95	24.25	0.00	2.51	1.25
1994	21.64	15.79	0.00	0.30	1.11
1995	29.12	55.53	0.00	4.54	1.01
1996	29.71	14.23	0.00	3.60	0.97

impressive gains in short periods, they can also fall just as quickly. Over the years, the performance of growth stocks has more than compensated for their fluctuations.

Figure 33.2 provides information on the T. Rowe Price Fund's performance from 1988 through 1996. It is based on a single share outstanding throughout each calendar year.

Costs of Investing

You pay no sales charges. All the money you invest in the fund goes to work for you, subject to transaction and fund expenses. These are costs you pay indirectly, because they are deducted from the fund's total assets. Following are transaction and fund expenses as of December 31, 1996.

Shareholder Transaction Expenses

Sales Charge (Load) on Purchases	None
Sales Charge (Load) on Reinvested Dividends	None
Redemption Fees	None
Exchange Fees	None

Annual Fund Expenses

Management Fee	0.66%
Marketing Fees (12b-1)	None
Other Expenses	0.31%
Total Fund Expenses	**0.97%**

Invest the Smart Way

Consider your investment goals, your time horizon for achieving them, and your tolerance for risk. If you seek an aggressive approach to capital growth, and can accept the above-average level of price fluctuations that science and technology funds are expected to experience, these funds could be an appropriate part of your overall investment strategy.

CHAPTER 34

Building Your Wealth in International Stock Funds

*I*nternational stock funds offer a way to diversify outside the U.S. in search of growth opportunities overseas. These funds seek long-term total return (capital appreciation and income) by investing in companies around the world. Today, many of the best investment opportunities may be found in foreign economies. Figure 34.1 lists the world's best-performing equity markets, in U.S. dollars, from 1976 through 1996.

If you already have a well-rounded portfolio of domestic stocks, bonds, and money-market securities, then diversifying with international investments can be a wise decision. Although international stocks have higher risk than U.S. stocks, combining the two in a portfolio may actually reduce your total portfolio risk. This potential benefit is achieved due to the fact that U.S. and foreign markets often move in opposite directions.

Non-U.S. stocks accounted for only 34 percent of worldwide stock values in 1970. Today, international stocks account for nearly 60 percent of the total value of stocks worldwide. Adding international stock funds to your portfolio allows you to participate in the many promising business opportunities that exist beyond U.S. borders.

Building international diversification into your mutual fund portfolio offers several benefits, but it can be daunting to sort through all the choices. To evaluate international stock funds, you should consider each one's geographic emphasis, strategy, cost, and past performance.

FIGURE 34.1   Best-Performing Equity Markets in U.S. Dollars

Year	Equity Market	Year	Equity Market	Year	Equity Market
1976	Hong Kong	1983	Norway	1990	United Kingdom
1977	United Kingdom	1984	Hong Kong	1991	Hong Kong
		1985	Austria		
1978	France	1986	Spain	1992	Hong Kong
1979	Norway	1987	Japan	1993	Hong Kong
1980	Italy	1988	Denmark	1994	Finland
1981	Sweden	1989	Austria	1995	Switzerland
1982	Sweden			1996	Brazil

You can choose from a broad selection of indexed and actively managed funds for investing abroad. (For an in-depth discussion of index funds, see Chapter 35). Each has a specific investment objective. For instance, some funds invest exclusively outside the United States, both in developed or emerging markets. There are also "world" or "global" funds that invest in securities worldwide, including the United States.

When you consider investing in international funds, keep these essentials in mind:

- Maintain a well-diversified portfolio of U.S. funds.
- Study funds that invest overseas, including their risk and reward characteristics.
- Consider the costs associated with any international fund investments.
- Decide which allocation and funds are most suitable for your long-range investment goals.

In addition to a prospectus and other information you can obtain by phone from each fund, helpful guidance is available from such mutual fund services as *Morningstar Mutual Funds* (800-735-0700) and *Value Line Mutual Fund Survey* (800-833-0046). These services may be found at many public libraries. They also offer trial subscriptions.

Now let's look at some specific fund groups you should consider as opportunities for building your wealth with international funds. The funds in each group are ranked in order of best average annual returns for the five years ending on March 31, 1997. You can obtain a prospectus and other information for each fund shown by calling the telephone number following the listing.

FIGURE 34.2 Top-Performing Europe Stock Funds (Average Annual Return for the Period Ending March 31, 1997)

Fund	3 Years	5 Years	Telephone
Dean Witter European Growth*	19.9%	19.7%	800-869-3863
Putnam Europe Growth A*	18.3	16.6	800-225-1581
Alliance New Europe A*	22.2	16.3	800-247-4154
T. Rowe Price European Stock	14.7	N/A	800-547-2308
Vanguard International Equity Index Fund European Portfolio	15.3	N/A	800-662-7447

*Indicates the fund charges a redemption fee or load.
N/A—Fund had not been in operation for five years.

International Stock Funds: Europe

Funds included in the Europe category seek long-term capital appreciation by investing in stocks, convertible bonds, and warrants traded on European stock exchanges, as well as American depositary receipts of European companies. Funds in this group tend to prefer exposure to the large, developed economies of western Europe, such as the United Kingdom, Germany, and France, rather than smaller peripheral countries, or the emerging markets of eastern Europe. The funds' returns usually show little correlation with the returns from U.S. stock exchanges. Note also that the fluctuation of European currency values has a considerable effect on total returns. Top-performing Europe stock funds are listed in Figure 34.2.

A Recommended Europe Stock Fund

Dean Witter European Growth Fund

Minimum initial investment: $1,000
Minimum subsequent investment: $100
Date of inception: May 31, 1990
Load: Redemption fee of up to 5 percent

FIGURE 34.3 Top-Performing Pacific Stock Funds (Average Annual Return For the Period Ending March 31, 1997)

Fund	3 Years	5 Years	Telephone
Putnam Asia Pacific Growth A*	1.2%	12.8%	800-225-1581
Hancock Pacific Basin A*	1.2	11.6	800-257-3336
GAM Pacific Basin A*	3.5	11.6	800-426-4685
Dean Witter Pacific Growth*	1.3	11.2	800-869-3863
Merrill Lynch Pacific A*	4.5	9.9	609-282-2800

*Indicates the fund charges a redemption fee or load.

Investment Objective

The fund seeks capital appreciation. It normally invests at least 65 percent of assets in securities issued in the British Isles, continental Europe, and Scandinavia. The fund tends to concentrate its investments in France, the United Kingdom, Germany, the Netherlands, Spain, Sweden, Switzerland, and Italy. The balance of assets may be invested in other countries, including the United States

Performance

If you had invested $10,000 for five years in Dean Witter European Growth Fund on November 1, 1991 (and reinvested income dividends and capital gains), it would have grown in five years to a value of $22,365 (on October 31, 1996).

International Stock Funds: Pacific

Diversified Pacific stock funds invest throughout the Pacific Rim. These funds usually have at least 65 percent of their assets invested in Asian stocks and at least 10 percent invested in Japanese securities. For the most part, these offerings are well diversified between Asia's more developed markets (Japan, Australia, and Hong Kong) and the region's emerging markets (such as Malaysia, Thailand, and the Philippines). Top-performing Pacific stock funds are listed in Figure 34.3.

A Recommended Pacific Stock Fund

Dean Witter Pacific Growth Fund

Minimum initial investment: $1,000
Minimum subsequent investment: $100
Date of inception: November 30, 1990
Load: Up to 5 percent redemption fee

Investment Objective

The fund seeks capital appreciation. The fund normally invests at least 65 percent of assets in securities issued by companies located in Asia, Australia, and New Zealand. It typically concentrates its investments in Japan and Hong Kong. The fund may invest up to 10 percent of assets in other investment companies.

Performance

If you had invested $10,000 in Dean Witter Pacific Growth Fund on December 1, 1991 (and reinvested income dividends and capital gains), it would have grown in five years to a value of $19,137 (on November 30, 1996).

International Stock Funds: Pacific Ex-Japan

Funds in the Pacific ex-Japan stock fund category invest mainly in the markets of Southeast Asia. Many of them also invest in South Asian markets, though to much less of an extent. Most of these funds keep their core holdings in Southeast Asia's most developed markets (Hong Kong, Singapore, and Malaysia), which contain some of the fastest growing economies in the world. However, the group as a whole is highly volatile; funds in this region have the potential both for dramatic gains and extreme losses. Top-performing Pacific ex-Japan stock funds are listed in Figure 34.4.

FIGURE 34.4 Top-Performing Pacific Ex-Japan Stock Funds (Average Annual Return for the Period Ending March 31, 1997)

Fund	3 Years	5 Years	Telephone
First Philippine CE	7.8%	20.7%	212-765-0700
Malaysia CE	7.5	13.7	800-221-6726
T. Rowe Price New Asia	4.6	11.9	800-638-5660
Asia Pacific CE	–4.1	9.7	800-225-1852

CE—Indicates a closed-end fund that trades on a stock exchange.

A Recommended Pacific Ex-Japan Stock Fund

Asia Pacific Fund

This closed-end fund trades on the New York Stock Exchange. Symbol: APB

Minimum initial investment: None
Minimum subsequent investment: None
Date of inception: May 5, 1987
Cost: Commission to buy and sell

Investment Objective

The fund seeks long-term capital appreciation. The fund normally invests at least 80 percent of assets in companies located in Hong Kong, Korea, Malaysia, the Philippines, Singapore, Taiwan, and Thailand. There is no limit to the percentage of assets that may be invested in any one country.

Performance

If you had invested $10,000 at the fund's inception on May 4, 1987 (and reinvested income dividends and capital gains), your shares would have grown in under ten years to a market value of $29,702 (on December 31, 1996). Shares of Asia Pacific Fund have experienced extreme volatility, as shown by the fund's total return to shareholders during the years from the fund's inception to the end of 1996:

FIGURE 34.5 Top-Performing Foreign Stock Funds (Average Annual Return for the Period Ending March 31, 1997)

Fund	3 Years	5 Years	Telephone
Hotchkis & Wiley International	13.2%	14.9%	800-236-4479
Managers International Equity	11.6	14.8	800-835-3879
Vanguard International Growth Portfolio	11.4	14.3	800-662-7447
Scudder International	9.0	11.6	800-225-2470
T. Rowe Price International Stock	12.2	10.1	800-638-5660

Year	Total Return	Year	Total Return
1987	−56.3%	1992	31.1%
1988	47.3	1993	106.6
1989	180.9	1994	−35.3
1990	−36.6	1995	4.5
1991	52.7	1996	−7.2

International Stock Funds: Foreign

Foreign stock funds invest in any country outside the United States. These funds are an ideal first stop if you are interested in diversifying a domestic U.S. portfolio. Funds in this group tend to invest the bulk of their assets in Japan and the developed markets of Europe. They may have limited exposure to emerging markets in Latin America, the Pacific, and other regions of the world (typically less than 25 percent of assets). See Figure 34.5 for top-performing funds in this group.

A Recommended Foreign Stock Fund

Vanguard International Growth Portfolio

Minimum initial investment: $3,000
Minimum subsequent investment: $100
Date of inception: September 30, 1981
Load: None

FIGURE 34.6   Top-Performing World Stock Funds (Average Annual
Return for the Period Ending March 31, 1997)

Fund	3 Years	5 Years	Telephone
Janus Worldwide	19.4%	18.8%	800-525-8983
New Perspective*	15.0	14.5	800-421-4120
Scudder Global	11.7	13.3	800-225-2470
Templeton Capital Accumulator*	12.2	10.1	800-638-5660
Robertson Stephens Contrarian	12.1	N/A	800-766-3863

*Fund charges a sales load.
N/A—Fund had not operated for five years.

Investment Objective

The fund seeks capital appreciation. Income is incidental. The
fund invests in a broadly diversified array of non-U.S. equity securities, primarily common stocks of seasoned companies.

Performance

If you had invested $10,000 in Vanguard International Growth
Portfolio on January 1, 1982 (and reinvested income dividends and
capital gains), at the end of 15 years (December 31, 1996) your
investment would have grown to a value of $95,712. By the end of
1996, $10,000 invested for five years would have grown to $18,098
and $10,000 invested for ten years would have grown to $26,112.

International Stock Funds: World

World stock funds (also called global stock funds) have few geographical limitations, and most divide assets among developed, emerging, and U.S. markets. This group has historically shown lower
volatility than other international stock categories. In recent years the
world stock fund category has enjoyed an advantage over its international peers because of its ability to invest in the powerful U.S. market.
For top-performing funds in this group, see Figure 34.6.

A Recommended World Stock Fund

New Perspective Fund

Minimum initial investment: $250
Minimum subsequent investment: $50
Date of inception: March 3, 1973
Load: 5.75 percent

Investment Objective

New Perspective Fund seeks long-term growth of capital. Potential for income is a secondary consideration. The fund invests primarily in the common stocks of foreign and U.S. companies. The manager looks for worldwide changes in international trade patterns and economic and political relationships. Securities, industries, governments, and currency-exchange markets worldwide are closely watched.

Performance

If you had invested $10,000 in New Perspective Fund on February 1, 1982 (and reinvested income dividends and capital gains), at the end of 15 years (January 31, 1997) your investment would have grown to a value of $96,843. On the same date in 1997, $10,000 invested for five years would have grown to $19,567 and $10,000 invested for ten years would have grown to $34,782.

Invest the Smart Way

You can use international stock funds in search of growth opportunities overseas. These funds seek long-term total return (capital appreciation and income) by investing in companies around the world. Although international stocks have higher risk than U.S. stocks, combining the two in a portfolio may actually reduce your total portfolio risk.

CHAPTER 35

Investing in the Whole Market—Index Funds

*I*nvestors have been rushing into index funds, which try to match the market rather than beat it. More than $8 billion of new money poured into the Vanguard Index Trust 500 Portfolio in 1996, a sum greater than the total assets of all but about 35 stock mutual funds.

You can now invest in a replication of the whole stock or bond market, or in specific segments of the market, by buying shares in a single fund. Any investor, even one with very limited funds, can invest in a fund that holds all 500 of the largest U.S. companies, a representation of small capitalization companies, a representation of the total U.S. stock market, a representation of the total U.S. bond market, or a representation of foreign stock markets, through an investment strategy known as indexing.

An increasing number of individual investors, pension funds, and institutional investors choose indexing. In 1994, according to the Vanguard Group of Investment Companies, the leading provider of index funds, individual investors owned some $10 billion in shares of index funds. By early 1997 this had ballooned to more than $60 billion. The Vanguard Group's own Index Trust 500 Portfolio, which replicates Standard & Poor's 500 Composite Stock Price Index, alone held net assets of more than $34 billion, making it the country's second-largest mutual fund.

Indexing describes the investment approach of attempting to parallel the investment returns of a specific stock or bond market index. A market index measures changes in the stock, bond, and commodities markets, reflecting market prices and the number of shares outstanding for the companies in the index. Well-known market indexes include the S&P 500, the Dow Jones Industrials, the New York Stock Exchange index, and the Wilshire 5000 index.

An index fund manager tries to replicate the target index investment results by holding all or a representative sample of the securities in the index. Indexing is a passive approach to investing. No attempt is made to use traditional active money management techniques in selecting individual stocks or industry sectors in an effort to outperform the indexes. The result is an investment approach emphasizing broad diversification and low portfolio trading activity.

Studies have shown that the stock market has had a long-term average return of about 10 percent per year. Some investors, as a result of luck or skill, have earned more than 10 percent; others have earned less. But the 10 percent historical return is the average amount that all investors can achieve as a group.

But that 10 percent is the gross return, before expenses (such as management fees, commissions, and other costs). The net return can be significantly less, resulting in a number well below the market return. Here's how it works: Most mutual funds have costs such as advisory fees, distribution charges, operating expenses, and portfolio transaction costs. According to Lipper Analytical Services, these costs, on average, total approximately 2 percent of investor assets. Thus, the net average return to investors is 8 percent, not the 10 percent provided by the market average.

In contrast, one key advantage of an index fund should be its low cost. A properly run index fund pays no advisory fees (because there is no active investment management), keeps operating expenses at a very low level, and keeps portfolio transaction costs at the minimum. The lower the expenses a fund incurs, the closer will be the fund's performance to the index it tracks.

Most professionally managed mutual funds underperform the market averages. Figure 35.1 shows the ten-year total return (capital change plus income) through December 31, 1996, of U.S. equity funds compared with the S&P 500 index (a measure representing about 80 percent of the market value of all issues traded on the New York Stock Exchange).

No group of U.S. general equity funds performed better on average than the S&P 500 index during the ten-year period. The average return of all U.S. equity funds was 13.30 percent—1.94 percentage points less than the unmanaged S&P 500, with dividends reinvested.

FIGURE 35.1   Ten-Year Average Annual Return Performance for the
Period Ending December 31, 1996 Annual

Objective	Return
Mid-Cap Funds	14.74%
Small Company Growth Funds	14.22
Growth Funds	13.47
Growth and Income Funds	13.13
Equity Income Funds	11.62
All Equity Funds as a Group	13.30
S&P 500 Index (With Dividends Reinvested)	**15.26**

Investing in Index Funds

An index fund invests in common stocks (or bonds) in an attempt to match the investment performance of a distinct market index. As a result, the fund achieves its goal over the long term. In 1996, according to the Vanguard Group, the S&P 500 index outperformed 75 percent of all actively managed equity mutual funds, with a total return of 23 percent. The index also outpaced the majority of equity funds in 16 of the 26 years from 1971 to 1996.

Indexing's main appeal is to long-term investors who seek a very competitive investment return through broadly diversified portfolios. Index funds provide investors with a high degree of relative predictability in an uncertain stock market. Nothing can ensure absolute returns, but these investors can feel confident that their investment should not be a dramatic underperformer relative to other funds investing in the same type of securities and, over the long term, index funds should deliver a very competitive relative performance.

You can now buy into the whole stock or bond market or into particular segments of the securities market. There is an increasing selection of indexes to choose from. Although most of the focus on index investing has been on funds that attempt to replicate the S&P 500, you can now find funds that seek to match other indexes, both in the U.S. market and abroad. Here are some of your choices:

- Dow Jones World Stock Index consists of approximately 2,600 stocks of U.S. and foreign companies, located in 25 countries. The index has approximately 120 industry groups and subgroups divided into nine broad market sectors.

- Lehman Brothers Aggregate Bond Index consists of more than 6,000 individual investment-grade, fixed-income securities, including U.S. Treasury and government agency securities, corporate debt obligations, and mortgage-backed securities.
- Morgan Stanley Capital International-Select Emerging Markets Free Index is a broadly diversified index consisting of approximately 460 common stocks of companies located in the countries of 12 emerging markets in Southeast Asia, Latin America, and Europe.
- Morgan Stanley Capital International Europe (Free) Index is a diversified index comprising approximately 575 companies located in 13 European countries. This index includes only the shares of companies that U.S. investors are "free to purchase."
- Morgan Stanley Capital International Pacific Index is a diversified index consisting of approximately 425 companies located in Australia, Japan, Hong Kong, New Zealand, and Singapore. The index is dominated by the Japanese stock market, which represents about 85 percent of its market capitalization.
- Morgan Stanley REIT Index is made up of the stocks of all publicly traded real estate investment trusts (REITs) that have a total market capitalization of at least $75 million and have enough shares and trading volume to be considered liquid. At the end of 1995, 93 equity REITs were included in the index.
- Russell 2000 Small Stock Index is a broadly diversified, small capitalization index consisting of approximately 2,000 common stocks. The average market capitalization of stocks in this index is about $200 million.
- S&P/BARRA Growth Index consists of stocks selected from the S&P 500 index with higher-than-average ratios of market price to book values.
- S&P/BARRA Value Index consists of stocks selected from the S&P 500 index with lower-than-average ratios of market price to book values.
- Standard & Poor's 500 index measures the total investment return of 500 common stocks, most of which trade on the NYSE and represent about 70 percent of the market value of all U.S. common stocks.
- Wilshire 4500 index consists of all U.S. stocks that are not in the S&P 500 index and that trade regularly on the NYSE and AMEX as well as in the Nasdaq OTC market. More than 5,000 stocks of midsized and small-capitalization companies are included in the index.

FIGURE 35.2   Total Return of Vanguard Index Trust 500 Portfolio 1981 to 1996 Compared with S&P 500

Year	Fund %	S&P 500 %	Year	Fund %	S&P 500 %	Year	Fund %	S&P 500 %
1981	−5.2	−4.9	1987	+4.7	+5.1	1993	+9.8	+10.1
1982	+20.9	+21.5	1988	+16.2	+16.6	1994	+1.1	+1.3
1983	+21.3	+22.5	1989	+31.3	+31.7	1995	+37.4	+37.6
1984	+6.2	+6.3	1990	−3.4	−3.1	1996	+22.9	+23.0
1985	+31.2	+31.8	1991	+30.2	+30.5			
1986	+18.0	+18.6	1992	+7.4	+7.6			

- Wilshire 5000 Index consists of all regularly and publicly traded U.S. stocks, providing a complete proxy for the U.S. stock market. More than 6,000 stocks, including large, medium-sized, and small-capitalization companies are included in the index. It represents the value of all NYSE, AMEX, and OTC stocks for which quotes are available.

Investors have wide-ranging interests and index funds are available for different market sectors. Figure 35.2 shows the total return achieved by the Vanguard Index Trust 500 Portfolio. This fund has been chosen for two reasons:

1. It is exceptionally well run, with low costs and a history of consistently coming very close to meeting its stated objective.
2. It replicates the S&P 500, which has attracted the most attention from investors interested in an index fund investment. Information about other no-load index funds is presented later in this chapter.

Only expenses separate Vanguard's 500 Portfolio from its target, the S&P 500. An index fund's expense ratio (advisory fees, operating expenses, and transaction costs) accounts for most of the difference between the fund's returns and those generated by its target index, so expenses are very important in assessing passively managed funds.

Other Mutual Funds and the Market Indexes They Target

Mutual fund companies have established more than 100 funds that track various market indexes, both in the United States and overseas. Because expenses account for most of the difference between an index fund's returns and those generated by the target index, you should carefully note the operating expenses of any index fund you are considering purchasing.

Following are a few no-load (or low-load) index funds and the indexes targeted by each fund.

Index Fund	Target Index
Dreyfus Corporation	
• People's Index Fund	S&P 500 index
• People's S&P Midcap Index Fund	S&P Midcap 400 Index
Fidelity Investments	
• Fidelity Market Index Fund	S&P 500 index
T. Rowe Price	
• T. Rowe Price Equity Index Fund	S&P 500 index
Charles Schwab	
• The Schwab International Index Fund	Schwab International Index
• The Schwab 1000 Fund	Schwab 1000 Index
SEI Financial Services	
• SEI S&P 500 Index Fund	S&P 500 index
The Vanguard Group of Investment Companies	
• Vanguard Balanced Index Fund	Wilshire 5000 Index & Lehman Brothers Aggregate Bond Index
• Vanguard Bond Index Fund Total Bond Market Portfolio	Lehman Brothers Aggregate Bond Index
• Short-Term Bond Portfolio	Lehman Brothers Mutual Fund Short (1–5) Government/ Corporate Index

- Intermediate-Term Bond Portfolio
  Lehman Brothers Mutual Fund Intermediate (5–10) Government/Corporate Index
- Long-Term Bond Portfolio
  Lehman Brothers Mutual Fund Long (10+) Government/ Corporate Index

Vanguard Index Trust
- Extended Market Portfolio — Wilshire 4500 Index
- 500 Portfolio — Standard & Poor's 500 Composite Stock Price Index
- Growth Portfolio — S&P/BARRA Growth Index
- Small Capitalization Stock Portfolio — Russell 2000 Small Stock Index
- Total Stock Market Portfolio — Wilshire 5000 Index
- Value Portfolio — S&P/BARRA Value Index

International Equity Index Fund
- Emerging Markets Portfolio — Morgan Stanley Emerging Markets Free Index
- European Portfolio — Morgan Stanley Europe (Free) Index
- Pacific Portfolio — Morgan Stanley Pacific Index

Invest the Smart Way

You can invest in the whole stock market, or important segments of it, by purchasing a single index fund. Over time certain market indexes, and funds that replicate them, have outperformed the majority of managed funds that have the same objective. Indexing has become the investment strategy of choice among many individual investors, as well as for many pension funds and institutional investors.

CHAPTER 36

Investing for Income in Bond Funds

Nearly everyone wants more income, whether to supplement what's already coming in, to accumulate assets for the future, or for some other purpose. Bond funds provide a simple and convenient way to meet this need. Cash assets, large or small, can be invested in funds whose only purpose is to deliver regular cash distributions.

In the early 1970s, the advent of the money-market mutual fund signaled a dramatic industry change. This new concept allowed the small investor to participate in the high short-term interest rates of money-market instruments that previously were available only to major institutions and the wealthy. Having previously used only bank savings accounts, many new investors learned the value of the mutual fund concept from money-market funds. The net asset value of each money-market fund has always remained at $1.

As in all investing, there are pitfalls to avoid. The investor should always remember that, as a general rule, the higher return, the greater the risk. There's just no way to get around this basic principle, although there are occasional exceptions.

No-Load versus Load Funds

One simple way to obtain a higher yield without increasing your risk is to select a bond fund with no sales charge or 12b-1 distribution fees and also one that has low annual expenses (a fund's charges are spelled

FIGURE 36.1 $10,000 Invested at $10 per Share (Net Asset Value) in
Bond Funds A and B

	Sales Charge*	Offering Price	Shares Bought
Bond Fund A	4.5%	$10.47	955.11
Bond Fund B	0.0	10.00	1,000.00

Income Distribution				
	Annual Expenses**	Income per Share	Annual Income	Yield
Bond Fund A	1.0%	$0.90	$859.60	8.6%
Bond Fund B	0.5	0.95	950.00	9.5

*As a percentage of the offering price.
**Both funds A & B are assumed to develop a 10 percent income from invested
assets, before expenses.

out clearly in the beginning of its prospectus). Assuming equivalent
management skills, investment objectives, and operating policies of the
bond funds under consideration, the result will be a higher distribution
of income to you. Figure 36.1 is an example of how this works for a
$10,000 investment.

It is clear from the illustration in Figure 36.1 that sales charges and
expense ratios can have a dramatic impact on mutual fund yields.

Tax-Free Bond Funds

Tax-free bond funds are generally offered in several levels of quality
and lengths of maturity. The quality relates to the creditworthiness of the
bonds in the portfolio, such as investment-grade, medium-grade, low-
grade (junk), or insured bonds. (For more information on how bonds are
rated, see Chapter 19.) Bonds are generally grouped by short-, interme-
diate-, and long-term maturities. The Vanguard Group, for example,
offers the Vanguard Municipal Bond Fund (800-662-7447), which
allows you to choose from several portfolios offering tax-free income
that is payable monthly:

- *Municipal Money-Market Portfolio.* This portfolio invests primarily in investment-grade municipal securities and expects to
  maintain an average weighted maturity of 120 days or less. The

NAV is expected to remain constant at $1 per share. Principal risk is minimal.

- *Municipal Bond Short-Term Portfolio.* This portfolio offers a high degree of capital stability with an average weighted maturity of one to two years. Price fluctuations and principal risk should be low.
- *Municipal Limited-Term Portfolio.* This portfolio seeks yields higher than those of short-term bonds but with less price volatility than long-term bonds. It invests in high-quality municipal bonds and expects to maintain an average weighted maturity of two to five years. Price fluctuations and principal risk should be moderate.
- *Municipal Bond Intermediate-Term Portfolio.* This portfolio invests in high-quality municipal bonds and expects to maintain an average maturity of 7 to 12 years. Price fluctuations and principal risk are moderate to high.
- *Municipal Insured Long-Term Portfolio.* This portfolio invests in high-quality municipal bonds that are covered by insurance guaranteeing the timely payment of principal and interest. The average weighted maturity is expected to be 20 to 25 years. Credit risk is virtually eliminated, but principal is subject to a high degree of price fluctuation.
- *Municipal Bond Long-Term Portfolio.* This portfolio invests in high-quality, long-term municipal bonds and expects to maintain an average weighted maturity of 20 to 25 years. There is high potential for price fluctuations and risk to principal.
- *Municipal Bond High-Yield Portfolio.* This portfolio invests primarily in medium-quality municipal bonds and expects to maintain an average weighted maturity of 20 to 25 years. This portfolio pursues the highest yields of the group and has a high potential for price fluctuations and risk to principal.

It is easy to get the current yields or annualized dividend distribution rates of any individual fund, either by calling the fund directly (usually on their toll-free number) or by looking it up yourself in a good financial periodical, such as *Barron's* or the *Wall Street Journal.*

To determine the current dividend distribution rate, simply multiply the last dividend paid by the number of payments made per year (usually 12) and divide that by the NAV per share. The distribution rates for the preceding Vanguard municipal bond fund portfolios on March 31, 1997, were as follows:

Fund	Distribution Rate
Municipal Money-Market Portfolio	3.3%
Municipal Bond Short-Term Portfolio	3.8
Municipal Limited-Term Portfolio	4.5
Municipal Bond Intermediate-Term Portfolio	5.1
Municipal Insured Long-Term Portfolio	5.5
Municipal Bond Long-Term Portfolio	5.4
Municipal Bond High-Yield Portfolio	5.6

Taxable Bond Funds

There is a diverse group of funds whose investment objectives are dedicated primarily to the development of current income that is not tax-exempt. They fall into two general categories:

1. Those holding securities issued or backed by the U.S. government (or its agencies)
2. Those issued by domestic corporations or foreign companies and governments

Some funds hold securities from both sectors. Each of the major mutual fund groups offers several types of funds where the primary investment objective is distribution of income.

For comparative illustration, a listing of several taxable bond funds offered by the Fidelity Distributors Corporation (800-544-8888) follow, along with their investment objectives.

Money-Market Funds

- *Cash Reserves.* This fund seeks to obtain as high a level of income as is consistent with the preservation of capital and liquidity. The fund invests in high-grade domestic and international money-market instruments.
- *Daily Income Trust.* The objective is the same for the Cash Reserves fund, except that it invests only in domestic money-market instruments.
- *Spartan Money.* This fund seeks the highest money-market yields wherever they may be. The fund invests in U.S. dollar-denominated money-market securities at home or overseas.
- *U.S. Government Reserves.* This fund seeks as high a level of income as is consistent with the security of principal and liquidity

by investing in instruments issued or guaranteed as to principal and interest by the U.S. government, its agencies, or instrumentalities. All investments are in obligations that mature in one year or less.

Fixed-Income Funds

- *Spartan High-Income.* This fund seeks to earn a high level of current income through investment in a diversified portfolio consisting primarily of high-yielding (lower-grade) fixed-income securities of all types.
- *Intermediate Bond.* This fund seeks a high level of current income by investing in high-grade fixed-income obligations. The portfolio will have an average maturity of three to ten years.
- *GNMA Portfolio.* This fund invests primarily in mortgage-related securities issued by the Government National Mortgage Association (GNMA) and other obligations guaranteed as to payment of principal and interest by the U.S. government. It seeks a high level of current income, consistent with prudent investment risk.
- *Government Securities.* This fund seeks a high level of current income consistent with preservation of capital. The fund invests only in U.S. government and government agency securities that provide interest that is specifically exempted from state and local income taxes when held directly by taxpayers.
- *Mortgage Securities.* This fund seeks a high level of current income consistent with prudent investment risk. It invests primarily in a broad range of mortgage-related securities issued by governmental, government-related, and private organizations.
- *Short-Term Bond Portfolio.* This fund seeks high current income consistent with preservation of capital by investing primarily in a broad range of investment-grade fixed-income securities. The fund will maintain an average maturity of three years or less.

All income distributions on these Fidelity taxable bond funds are payable monthly. Their dividend distribution rates (yields) as of March 31, 1997, were as follows:

Fund	Yield
Cash Reserves	5.13%
Daily Income Trust	5.01
Spartan Money	5.13

U.S. Government Reserves	5.13
Spartan High-Income	8.40
Intermediate Bond	6.60
GNMA Portfolio	6.70
Government Securities	7.00
Mortgage Securities	6.50
Short-Term Bond Portfolio	6.50

Funds offered by other mutual fund groups having investment objectives that match the preceding funds will have similar yields. While there can be some differences in managements' ability to acquire securities efficiently, and thus increase yield, the most effective ways for a fund to produce a higher field is by controlling its costs or by purchasing lower-quality securities. (Generally speaking, the less creditworthy a security is, the higher will be its yield.)

High-Yielding No-Load Bond Funds

Figure 36.2 shows top-performing no-load taxable bond funds at the end of March 1997, ranked in order of best five-year total return (income plus change in value) in each of several investment objective categories where income is primary. Funds with annual 12b-1 fees exceeding 0.25 percent are not included.

Invest the Smart Way

*I*f you are seeking income, whether to supplement what's already coming in, to accumulate assets for the future, or for some other purpose, bond funds provide a simple and convenient way to meet this need. Your cash assets, large or small, can be invested in funds whose only purpose is to deliver regular cash distributions. To obtain a higher yield without increasing your risk, select a bond fund with no sales charge or 12b-1 distribution fees and also one that has low annual expenses.

FIGURE 36.2   Top-Performing No-Load Taxable Bond Funds by
Investment Objective on March 31, 1997

Fund	Current Yield	5-Year Total Return	Telephone
Long-Term Bond Funds			
Vanguard Preferred Stock	6.9%	9.2%	800-662-7447
Vanguard Fixed-Income Long-Term Corporate Bond	7.2	8.6	800-662-7447
Vanguard Fixed-Income Long-Term U.S. Treasury	6.8	8.6	800-662-7447
Invesco Select Income	7.3	8.5	800-525-8085
USAA Income	7.0	7.5	800-531-8181
Intermediate-Term Government Bond Funds			
Heartland U.S. Government Securities	6.4	7.6	800-432-7856
Vanguard Fixed-Income Intermediate-Term U.S. Treasury	6.4	7.4	800-662-7447
Fidelity Mortgage Securities	6.5	7.2	800-544-8888
Vanguard Fixed-Income GNMA	7.1	6.9	800-662-7447
USAA GNMA	7.0	6.9	800-531-8181
Intermediate-Term Bond Funds			
Strong Corporate Bond	6.8	10.5	800-368-1030
T. Rowe Price Spectrum Income	6.4	8.8	800-638-5660
Stein Rowe Income	7.4	8.3	800-338-2550
Strong Government Securities	6.2	8.2	800-368-1030
Harbor Bond	6.8	8.1	800-422-1050
High-Yield Bond Funds			
Northeast Investors	8.9	14.7	800-225-6704
Fidelity Spartan High-Income	8.4	13.4	800-544-8888
Fidelity Capital and Income	8.3	11.6	800-544-8888
Vanguard Fixed-Income High Yield Corporate	8.9	10.6	800-662-7447
Federated High Yield	9.4	10.5	800-341-7400
International Bond Funds			
Warburg Pincus Global Fixed-Income	8.5	9.2	800-927-2874
T. Rowe Price International Bond	5.9	9.0	800-638-5660
American Century—Benham European Government Bond	4.5	9.0	800-345-2021
Scudder Emerging Markets Income	9.1	19.1*	800-225-2470
Legg Mason Global Government	6.6	8.7*	800-822-5544

*Three-year total return. Fund not in operation for five years.

CHAPTER 37

Funds You Can Buy at a Discount

*I*nvestment companies also sponsor closed-end funds, which, unlike open-end mutual funds, do not stand ready to issue and redeem shares on a continuous basis. Instead, closed-end funds have a fixed capitalization represented by shares that are publicly traded, usually on major stock exchanges. The total market valuation of closed-end funds in 1997 was about $110 billion, compared to $3.2 *trillion* in open-end funds. One interesting and potentially profitable aspect of closed-end funds is that they are often available for purchase at a discount from their net asset value.

Like open-end funds, closed-end funds operate by pooling the funds of shareholders and investing those funds in a diversified securities portfolio having a specified investment objective. The funds provide professional management, economies of scale, and the liquidity available with public trading on a major exchange. While the NAV of closed-end funds is calculated the same way as for open-end funds, the price an investor will pay or receive for shares traded on an exchange may be above or below the NAV. This is because the price of shares is determined on an auction market basis, the same as for all other traded shares of stock. Thus, the investor in a closed-end fund has an additional tier of risk, and possible profit, that the open-end fund investor does not have. The value per share responds not only to the fluctuation in value of the underlying securities in the fund's portfolio, but also to supply and demand factors that influence the fund's share price as it trades on an exchange.

Closed-end funds frequently have specialized portfolios of securities and may be oriented toward current income, long-term growth of capital, or a combination of objectives. For instance, the Argentina Fund seeks capital appreciation by investing in equity securities of companies that mainly do business in Argentina. It trades on the New York Stock Exchange. Another example is the CIM High-Yield Securities Fund, which also trades on the NYSE and seeks a high level of income by investing in lower than investment-grade bonds.

Closed-end funds hold two main attractions for investors:

1. Management of a closed-end fund is not concerned with continuous buying and selling of securities in its portfolio to accommodate new investors and redemptions, as is the responsibility of an open-end fund, and which may conflict with ideal market timing. Thus, a well-managed closed-end fund can often buy and sell on more favorable terms.
2. Shares of closed-end funds are frequently available for purchase at a discount from net asset value—something never possible with open-end mutual funds.

The resulting benefit of these two factors is that annual earnings of investors in closed-end funds sometimes exceed the earnings of open-end funds with similar portfolios.

Shares of closed-end funds are purchased and sold through securities brokers. Commissions, which vary from broker to broker, are payable both when shares are purchased and again when they are sold. Typically, shares are traded in 100-share lots, but "odd lots" of fewer than 100 shares may also be transacted.

The price, or market value, of closed-end shares is determined by supply and demand factors affecting the market. Shares may trade at a premium or at a discount relative to the NAV of the fund. Factors at work in determining share price include the composition of the portfolio, yield, the general market, and year-end tax selling. Some funds have buyback programs designed to support the market price, reduce the number of shares outstanding, and increase earnings per share. When shares are first issued, they tend to sell at a premium for a time, then fall back when brokers stop aggressively promoting them and turn their attention to other products.

According to Lipper Analytical Services, about 82 percent of the nation's 510 closed-end funds traded at a discount in mid-1996, with equity funds trading at an average 13 percent discount to NAV. This contrasted with 1992 and 1993 when investors frequently paid a premium to buy closed-end fund shares.

In addition to daily transactions of closed-end funds contained in the financial sections of major newspapers, *Barron's* includes a special section each week with a complete listing of closed-end funds. Closed-end funds selling at a premium or discount to NAV are also listed separately once a week in *The New York Times* and in *The Wall Street Journal.*

Morningstar Closed-End Funds (800-735-0700), a biweekly investment service, provides detailed information and source material on more than 350 closed-end funds.

Types of Closed-End Funds

Like open-end mutual funds, closed-end funds may be divided into various general classifications. In the section that follows, several closed-end funds are presented within each classification showing where they trade, the NAV and market price of each, and the discount each traded at on February 14, 1997. Also shown are 52-week market returns for equity funds (not including dividends). Current dividend yields are shown for bond funds. The examples shown illustrate the variation in share prices to NAVs. Each fund is shown with the exchange on which it trades: A = American, N = NYSE, O = Nasdaq.

General Equity Funds

General equity funds seek capital appreciation. They normally invest in the common stocks of well-established companies, with the aim of producing an increase in the value of their investments rather than a flow of dividends. Investors who buy shares of closed-end general equity funds are usually more interested in seeing share prices rise than in receiving income from dividends. Figure 37.1 provides data on funds in the general equity group selling at a discount from their NAVs on February 14, 1997.

Specialized Equity Funds

This group includes funds that primarily confine their investments to securities in certain sectors of the market, such as utilities, precious metals, emerging markets, natural resources, health care, and so on.

FIGURE 37.1   General Equity Funds Selling at a Discount (February 14, 1997)

Name of Fund	Stock Exchange	NAV	Market Price	Discount	52-Week Market Return
Adams Express	N	$ 25.20	20⅞	−17.2%	16.8%
Baker Fentress	N	22.53	18	−20.1	15.9
Bergstrom Capital	A	146.26	122⅝	−16.2	11.4
Engex	A	16.49	11½	−30.3	−7.1
General American	N	25.84	21¾	−15.8	20.5

Because of the diversity of their objectives, with some funds seeking income and others seeking growth of capital, total return comparisons are not always meaningful. Figure 37.2 shows specialized equity funds selling at a discount from their NAVs on February 14, 1997.

World Equity Funds

Funds in this group generally confine their portfolios to the common stock of companies located in one country or region, although the investment objectives of some funds permit them to invest anywhere in the world. Figure 37.3 shows world equity funds selling at a discount to their NAVs on February 14, 1997.

FIGURE 37.2   Specialized Equity Funds Selling at a Discount (February 14, 1997)

Name of Fund	Stock Exchange	NAV	Market Price	Discount	52-Week Market Return
Alliance Global Environmental	N	17.40	14¼	−18.1%	38.3%
H&Q Health Investors	N	23.30	18¼	−21.7	0.0
Pilgrim America Bank & Thrift	N	19.80	17⅞	−9.7	59.7
Southeastern Thrift	O	19.09	18⅝	−2.4	39.6

FIGURE 37.3   World Equity Funds Selling at a Discount (February 14, 1997)

Name of Fund	Stock Exchange	NAV	Market Price	Discount	52-Week Market Return
Asia Pacific	N	$14.83	12½	−15.7%	−16.1%
Austria Fund	N	11.54	9⅛	−20.9	1.4
Central European Equity	N	27.48	22⅞	−16.8	41.6
Germany Fund	N	15.97	12¾	−20.2	18.6

Dual-Purpose Funds

A special form of closed-end fund is the dual-purpose fund. This type of fund contains two classes of stock. Common shareholders receive all capital gains realized on the sale of securities in the fund's portfolio. Preferred shareholders receive all the dividend and interest income from the portfolio. Dual-purpose funds have a specific expiration date, when preferred shares are redeemed at a predetermined price and common shareholders claim the remaining assets. They then vote either to liquidate or to continue the fund on an open-end basis. Figure 37.4 shows two dual-purpose funds selling at a discount to their net asset values on February 14, 1997.

Convertible Securities Funds

Funds in this group generally invest in bonds, notes, debentures, and, to some extent, preferred stock that can be exchanged for a set number of shares of common stock in the issuing company at a prestated price or exchange ratio. As such, they have characteristics similar to both fixed-income and equity securities. Figure 37.5 shows convertible securities funds selling at a discount on February 14, 1997.

FIGURE 37.4   Dual Purpose Funds Selling at a Discount (February 14, 1997)

Name of Fund	Stock Exchange	NAV	Market Price	Discount	52-Week Market Return
Gemini II Capital	N	$30.73	30¼	−1.6%	22.0%
Quest for Value Cap	N	37.23	36¼	−2.6	9.4

FIGURE 37.5   Convertible Securities Funds Selling at a Discount (February 14, 1997)

Name of Fund	Stock Exchange	NAV	Market Price	Discount	52-Week Market Return
Bancroft Convertible	N	$27.39	23½	−14.2%	14.2%
Castle Convertible	A	28.91	26	−10.1	11.9
Ellsworth Convertible	A	11.56	10	−12.5	16.3
Lincoln Convertible	N	19.85	19¼	−3.0	30.9

Fixed-Income Funds

Closed-end fixed-income funds seek income for their shareholders by purchasing fixed-income securities issued by corporations and/or the U.S. government or its agencies, depending on the investment objectives spelled out in their charters. Funds in this group represent a wide range of risk categories, with some portfolios holding mainly high-yield "junk" bonds and others emphasizing investment-quality instruments. Figure 37.6 illustrates fixed-income funds selling at a discount on February 14, 1997, with their current income yield.

FIGURE 37.6   Fixed-Income Funds Selling at a Discount (February 14, 1997)

Name of Fund	Stock Exchange	NAV	Market Price	Discount	52-Week Market Return
ACM Government Securities	N	$10.34	9¼	−10.5%	8.9%
Allmerica Securities	N	11.63	10⅛	−10.8	8.5
Heritage U.S. Government	N	11.99	11⅝	−3.0	9.3
Highlander Income	A	14.26	12½	−12.3	8.9
Mentor Income	N	10.08	9	−10.7	9.3

FIGURE 37.7 World Income Funds Selling at a Discount (February 14, 1997)

Name of Fund	Stock Exchange	NAV	Market Price	Discount	52-Week Market Return
Dreyfus Strategic Government	N	$10.71	9¼	−13.6%	9.0%
Emerging Markets Income	N	20.61	18¼	−11.5	11.6
First Commonwealth	N	14.17	12	−15.3	8.4
Salomon SBW	N	17.17	15⅛	−11.9	10.0
Strategic Global Income	N	14.50	12½	−13.8	9.2

World Income Funds

World income funds invest in the debt securities of companies and countries worldwide, including the United States. They seek to provide current income for their shareholders. Figure 37.7 shows world income funds selling at a discount on February 14, 1997, with their current income yield.

National Municipal Bond Funds

Funds in this group invest in bonds issued by states and municipalities to finance schools; highways; airports; bridges; hospitals; water and sewer works; and other public projects. In most cases, income earned from these securities is exempt from federal income tax but may be subject to state and local taxes. Figure 37.8 illustrates national municipal bond funds selling at a discount on February 14, 1997, with their current dividend yield.

FIGURE 37.8   National Municipal Bond Funds Selling at a Discount (February 14, 1997)

Name of Fund	Stock Exchange	NAV	Market Price	Discount	52-Week Market Return
American Municipal Income	N	$14.15	12⅜	−12.5%	6.2%
Black Rock Insured Municipal	N	10.99	10⅜	−5.6	6.2
Colonial Investment Grade	N	10.96	10¼	−6.5	6.1
Insured Municipal Income	N	14.78	12⅜	−8.0	6.3
Municipal Partners	N	14.14	12⅛	−14.3	6.5

Invest the Smart Way

Closed-end fund shares are traded in the securities markets, with prices determined by supply and demand, making it possible for investors to have the frequent opportunity to buy shares at a discount from net asset value. This can result in yields and total annual returns that sometimes exceed the earnings of open-end funds with similar portfolios.

CHAPTER 38

The New Mutual Fund Supermarkets

*F*und shopping networks are among the newest and most convenient services available to mutual fund investors through discount brokers. These networks enable you to buy and sell a wide range of mutual funds through one source. When you invest through one of these one-stop sources, you can choose from more than 1,100 no-load mutual funds, sponsored by many of America's leading fund companies, and pay no transaction fee. And the number continues to grow. According to Don Phillips, vice president of Morningstar, Inc., the networks will become the dominant way to distribute mutual funds.

The basic idea is simple: You can buy and sell shares in numerous mutual funds without paying a transaction fee. You can buy funds for the same cost as going to the individual fund companies. And when you select no-load funds, paying no sales commissions or fees, you're putting the full value of your dollars to work in your investments. Transaction fees are charged on certain no-load funds, generally those that have chosen not to participate in the program. In addition, hundreds of load funds also can be purchased in some programs, in which case you will be charged the sales load as described in the prospectus. Business can be transacted with a telephone call, and everything is clearly summarized on one statement.

The two biggest programs in terms of assets are Charles Schwab's Mutual Fund OneSource, with more than $10 billion under management, and Fidelity Investment's FundsNetwork, with $5 billion. Other companies offering similar plans include Jack White & Company, Muriel Siebert & Company, and Waterhouse Securities.

How One-Stop Shopping Plans Work for You

You pay no loads or transaction fees to invest in a wide range of no-load funds available from different fund companies. The price you pay is exactly the same as investing directly with the fund itself.

Whatever your investment objective, from capital preservation to aggressive growth, a one-source mutual fund service gives you a nearly complete range of funds to choose from to help you reach your objective. You can move easily between funds, even if they're from different fund companies. This way, you can adjust your mutual fund portfolio to reflect changing investment goals or market conditions.

Once you have established an account, you can invest in hundreds of mutual funds with a single phone call. Some firms offer limited commission-free trading and will permit you to buy funds on margin or sell short, two highly speculative trading techniques. (For more on this, see Chapter 9.)

Because fund companies pay to participate, organizations that offer no-transaction-fee mutual fund network services are compensated by fees received directly from the fund companies. These fees range from 0.20 percent to 0.35 percent of the assets managed by the program. As long as these costs are not passed along to shareholders and fund expense ratios stay at reasonable levels, this should not be a problem to investors.

Although the general approaches for companies providing one-stop shopping plans are straightforward and pretty much the same, there are some differences. To get started you must first open a discount brokerage account with the firm of your choice. This gives you access to the mutual fund network plus the opportunity to trade in stocks, bonds, and other securities. Then, to purchase shares, instruct your representative about the name of the fund, the dollar amount you want to invest, and whether you want fund dividends and capital gains paid in cash or automatically reinvested in more fund shares. To sell, you need only specify the fund, the number of shares you wish to sell, and whether you want to receive the proceeds or have them credited to your account.

The fund consolidators (mutual fund one-source discount brokers) maintain single, multimillion-dollar accounts at the mutual fund families, so they have some flexibility on minimum investment requirements. Schwab's Mutual Fund OneSource program, for instance, has minimums that range from $250 to $2,000, which in some cases is below what you would have to invest when dealing directly with a fund.

One problem with the one-stop shopping system is that several excellent fund families, including T. Rowe Price, USAA, and Vanguard don't participate in some of the "free" programs. However, they are available if a transaction fee is paid. The Vanguard Group, for instance, has its own one-stop shopping system under which a fixed service fee is charged for each order (except for Vanguard Fund orders, which incur no fee or load). Generally, firms offering the program will let you transfer most outside funds into your consolidated account, at no extra cost. This way you can easily keep track of your holdings.

The Major Players

Following are the major discount brokers that offer one-stop mutual fund shopping programs. Prices and rules vary somewhat between firms, so contact the broker for full information.

Fidelity Investments
161 Devonshire Street
Boston, MA 02110
800-544-9697

Service: FundsNetwork

Charles Schwab & Co., Inc.
101 Montgomery Street
San Francisco, CA 94104
800-566-5623

Service: Mutual Fund OneSource

Muriel Siebert & Co., Inc.
885 Third Avenue
New York, NY 10022-4834
800-872-0666

Service: FundExchange

The Vanguard Group
P.O. Box 2600
Valley Forge, PA 19482
800-992-8327

Service: FundAccess

Waterhouse Securities, Inc.
100 Wall Street
New York, NY 10005
800-934-4443

Service: Mutual FundConnection

Jack White & Company
9191 Towne Centre Drive
San Diego, CA 92122
800-216-2333

Service: Mutual Fund Network/NoFee Network

Invest the Smart Way

Consider using a discount broker's mutual fund network. One-stop fund shopping is one of the newest and most beneficial services available to investors. You can choose from hundreds of mutual funds through one source with a single phone call, often without paying any fee or commission.

GLOSSARY

accumulation plan An arrangement whereby an investor makes voluntary purchases of mutual fund shares in large or small amounts.

adviser *See* investment management company.

American depositary receipts (ADRs) Receipts for the shares of a foreign-based corporation held in the vault of a U.S. bank and entitling the shareholder to all dividends and capital gains, thus eliminating the need to buy shares of those foreign-based companies in overseas markets.

appreciation The increase in the value of an asset such as a stock, bond, or mutual fund.

asked price The price at which the buyer may purchase shares of a security.

at the market An order to buy or sell a security at the best available price.

back-end load A redemption fee charged to an investor in certain mutual funds when shares are redeemed within a specified number of years after purchase.

balanced fund A mutual fund that at all times holds bonds, preferred stocks, or both, in varying ratios to common stocks to maintain relatively greater stability of both capital and income.

basis The cost an investor uses to calculate capital gains when selling a stock, bond, or mutual fund.

bid price The highest price a prospective buyer is prepared to pay for a security at a particular time.

blue chip The common stock of large, well-known companies with a relatively stable record of earnings and dividend payments over many years.

bond An interest-bearing or discounted government or corporate security that obligates the issuer to pay the bondholder a specified sum of money, usually at specific intervals, and to repay the principal amount of the loan at maturity.

bond rating A method of evaluating the possibility of default by a bond issuer.

break-point In the purchase of mutual fund shares, the dollar value level at which the percentage of the sales charge becomes lower. A sales charge schedule typically contains five or six break-points.

book value The net asset value of a company's securities.

bull A person who thinks prices will rise.

bull market A prolonged rise in the prices of stocks, bonds, or commodities.

buying on margin Buying securities with credit through a margin account held with a broker.

call An issuer's right to redeem bonds or preferred stock before maturity.

capital (1) The assets of a business, including plant and equipment, inventories, cash, and receivables. (2) The financial assets of an investor.

capital gains Profits realized from the sale of securities.

capital gains distribution A distribution to shareholders from net capital gains realized by a mutual fund on the sale of portfolio securities.

cash equivalent Includes short-term U.S. government securities, short-term commercial paper, and short-term municipal and corporate bonds and notes; money-market mutual funds.

certificates of deposit (CDs) Interest-bearing certificates issued by banks or savings and loan associations against funds deposited in the issuing institutions.

closed-end fund An investment company with a relatively fixed amount of capital and whose shares are traded on a securities exchange or in the over-the-counter market.

commercial paper Short-term, unsecured promissory notes issued by corporations to finance short-term credit needs. The maturity at the time of issuance normally does not exceed nine months.

common stock A security representing ownership of a corporation's assets. The right to common stock dividends comes after the requirements of bonds and preferred stocks.

convertible securities Securities carrying the right to exchange the security for other securities of the issuer (under certain conditions). This normally applies to preferred stock or bonds carrying the right to exchange for given amounts of common stock.

debenture A bond secured only by the general credit of the corporation.

discount The percentage below net asset value at which the shares of a closed-end fund sell.

distributions Dividends paid from net investment income and payments made from realized capital gains.

diversification Investment in a number of different security issues for the purpose of spreading and reducing the risks that are inherent in all investing.

diversified investment company A company that, under the Investment Company Act, in respect to 75 percent of its total assets, has invested not more than 5 percent of its total assets in any one company and holds not more than 10 percent of the outstanding voting securities of any one company.

dividend A payment from income on a share of common or preferred stock.

dollar cost averaging A method of automatic capital accumulation that provides for regular purchases of equal dollar amounts of securities and results in an average cost per share lower than the average price at which purchases have been made.

dual-purpose fund A type of closed-end mutual fund that is designed to serve the needs of two distinct types of investors: (1) those interested only in income and (2) those interested only in possible capital gains. It has two separate classes of shares.

earnings In respect to common stock, a company's net income after all charges (including preferred dividend requirements) divided by the number of common shares outstanding.

equity securities The securities in a corporation that represent ownership of the company's assets (generally common stocks).

exchange privilege The right to exchange the shares of one open-end mutual fund for those of another within the same fund group at a nominal charge (or at no charge) or at a reduced sales charge.

expense ratio The proportion that annual expenses, including all costs of operation, bear to average net assets for the year.

first in, first out (FIFO) An accounting method for determining cost basis that assumes the first shares sold are the first shares purchased.

fixed-income security A preferred stock or debt instrument with a stated percentage or dollar income return.

front-end load A sales fee charged investors in certain mutual funds at the time shares are purchased.

general obligation bonds Bonds that are backed by the full taxing power of a state or municipality.

government agency issues Debt securities issued by government-sponsored enterprises, federal agencies, and international institutions. Such securities are not direct obligations of the U.S. Treasury but involve government guarantees or sponsorship.

growth stock A stock that has shown better-than-average growth in earnings and is expected to continue to do so as a result of additional resources, new products, or expanded markets.

income The total amount of dividends and interest received from a fund's investments before deduction of any expenses.

income fund A mutual fund whose primary objective is current income.

individual retirement account (IRA) A tax-saving retirement program for individuals, established under the Employee Retirement Security Act of 1974.

inflation Persistent upward movement in the general price level of goods and services that results in a decline in the purchasing power of money.

investment adviser *See* investment management company.

investment company A corporation or trust through which investors pool their money to obtain supervision and diversification of their investments (mutual fund).

investment management company An organization employed by a mutual fund to give professional advice on the fund's investments and asset management practices (also called *adviser* or *investment adviser*).

investment objective The goal of an investor or investment company. It may be growth of capital and income, current income, relative stability of capital, or some combination of these aims.

investment policies The means or management techniques that an investment manager employs in an attempt to achieve the stated investment objective.

joint tenants An asset ownership arrangement by two or more persons in which each owner holds an equal share. At death, an owner's share is divided equally among the surviving co-owners.

Keogh plan A tax-favored retirement program for self-employed persons and their employees.

leverage In securities, a means of enhancing return or value without increasing investment. An example of leverage is buying securities on margin.

liquid assets Assets that are easily converted into cash or exchanged for other assets.

liquidity Assets are said to have liquidity when they can be easily converted into cash or exchanged for other assets.

load *See* sales charge.

low-load Indicates that the load (sales fee) charged to investors in certain mutual funds is no greater than 3 percent of the amount invested.

management company *See* investment management company.

management fee The charge made to an investment company for supervision of its portfolio. It frequently includes various other services and is usually a fixed or reducing percentage of average assets at market value.

money-market fund A mutual fund whose investments are in short-term debt securities, designed to maximize current income with liquidity and capital preservation.

municipal bond fund A mutual fund that invests in diversified holdings of tax-exempt securities, the income from which is exempt from federal taxes.

mutual fund *See* open-end investment company.

National Association of Securities Dealers (NASD) An organization of brokers and dealers in the over-the-counter securities market that administers rules of fair practice and rules to prevent fraudulent acts for the protection of the investing public.

net asset value (NAV) NAV equals the total assets of a mutual fund at market value, less current liabilities.

no-load fund A mutual fund selling its shares at net asset value without any sales charges.

offering price *See* asked price.

open-end investment company An investment company whose shares are redeemable at any time at approximate net asset value.

option A right to buy or sell specific securities at a specified price within a specified period of time.

over-the-counter (OTC) A market in which securities transactions are conducted through a telephone and computer network connecting dealers in stocks and bonds, rather than on the floor of an exchange.

par value The nominal or face value of a security.

payout ratio The percentage of a firm's profits that is paid out to shareholders in the form of dividends.

performance *See* management record.

portfolio The securities owned by an investment company.

portfolio turnover The dollar value of purchases and sales of portfolio securities, not including transactions in U.S. government obligations and commercial paper.

preferred stock An equity security, generally carrying a fixed dividend, whose claim to earnings and assets must be paid before common stock is entitled to share.

premium The percentage above net asset value (NAV) at which the shares of a closed-end fund trade.

price-earnings (PE) ratio The price of a stock divided by its earnings per share over a 12-month period.

principal amount The face value of a bond that must be repaid at maturity, as distinguished from interest.

prospectus A formal written offer to sell securities that sets forth the plan for a proposed business enterprise or mutual fund, or the facts about an existing one that an investor needs to make an informed decision.

real estate investment trust (REIT) A company that owns and manages a portfolio of real estate properties, mortgages, or both.

redemption price *See* bid price.

registered investment company An investment company that has filed a registration statement with the Securities and Exchange Commission (SEC) under the requirements of the Investment Company Act of 1940.

regulated investment company An investment company that has elected to qualify for the special tax treatment provided by Subchapter M of the Internal Revenue Code.

reinvestment privilege A service offered by most mutual funds and some common stocks and closed-end funds through which dividends from investment income may be automatically invested in additional full and fractional shares.

retained earnings Net profits kept to accumulate in a business after dividends are paid.

sales charge An amount that, when added to the net asset value (NAV) of mutual fund shares, determines the offering price. It covers commissions and other costs and is generally stated as a percentage of the offering price.

Securities and Exchange Commission (SEC) An independent agency of the U.S. government that administers the various federal securities laws.

selling short The sale of a stock, not owned by the seller, in the hope of buying it back at a lower price. The stock is borrowed by the seller at the time of the short sale.

statement of additional information Contains more complete information than is found in a prospectus and is on file with the Securities and Exchange Commission.

stock The ownership of a corporation represented by shares that are a claim on the corporation's earnings and assets.

stock dividend The payment of a corporate dividend in the form of stock rather than cash.

stockholder of record A common or preferred stockholder whose name is registered on the books of a corporation as owning shares as of a particular date.

stock symbol Letters used to identify listed companies on the securities exchanges on which they trade.

street name A phrase describing securities held in the name of a broker or another nominee instead of a customer.

tenants in common A type of asset ownership for two or more persons in which, upon the death of one owner, his or her share passes to heirs if a will is left or to the estate if no will is left, rather than to the co-owners.

ticker tape A device that relays the stock symbol and the latest price and volume on securities as they are traded to investors around the world.

total return A statistical measure of performance reflecting the reinvestment of both capital gains and income dividends.

Treasury bill A noninterest-bearing security issued by the U.S. Treasury and sold at a discount, with a maturity of one year or less.

treasury direct A system through which an investor can invest in U.S. Treasury securities through Federal Reserve Banks, bypassing banks or broker-dealers and avoiding their fees.

turnover ratio The extent to which an investment company's portfolio (exclusive of U.S. government obligations and commercial paper) is turned over during the course of a year.

12b-1 fee The fee charged by some funds, permitted under a 1980 Securities and Exchange Commission rule (for which it is named), to pay for distribution costs such as advertising or for commissions paid to brokers.

unrealized appreciation or depreciation The amount by which the market value of a portfolio's holdings exceeds or falls short of its cost.

U.S. government securities   Various types of marketable securities issued by the U.S. Treasury, consisting of bills, notes, and bonds.

volatility   The relative rate at which a security or fund shares tends to move up or down in price as compared with some market index.

withdrawal plan   An arrangement provided by many mutual funds by which an investor can receive periodic payments in a designated amount, which may be more or less than the actual investment income.

yield   Income received from investments, usually expressed as a percentage of the market price.

yield to maturity   The rate of return on a debt security held to maturity. Both interest payments and capital gain or loss are taken into account.

zero-coupon security   A security that makes no periodic interest payments but instead is sold at a deep discount from its face value.

INDEX